the dictionary of (bull•shit)

A shamelessly opinionated guide
to all that is absurd, misleading
and insincere

Nick Webb

SOURCEBOOKS, INC.®
NAPERVILLE, ILLINOIS

Published by Sourcebooks, Inc.
P.O. Box 4410, Naperville, Illinois 60567–4410
(630) 961–3900
Fax: (630) 961–2168
www.sourcebooks.com

Originally published: Great Britain : Robson Books, 2005.

Library of Congress Cataloging-in-Publication Data

Webb, Nick
  The dictionary of bullshit : a shamelessly opinionated guide to all that is absurd, misleading and insincere / Nick Webb.— [American ed.].
     p. cm.
  ISBN-13: 978-1-4022-0780-8
  ISBN-10: 1-4022-0780-8
  1. English language—United States—Terms and phrases. 2. English language—United States—Usage—Dictionaries. 3. English language—United States—Jargon—Dictionaries. 4. Business—United States—Dictionaries. I. Title.

PE1689.W43 2006
423'.1—dc22

                                                                        2006007112

Printed and bound in the United States
LB 10 9 8 7 6 5 4 3 2 1

For Susan and Catherine

contents

Acknowledgments

Many people have helped me to compile this book by suggesting examples of irritating bullshit. The expressions of relief on their faces when they unburden themselves suggest that many of us are tormented by bullshit, but find it expedient to keep quiet. I am grateful to them all for their time and generosity. The errors of analysis, attribution, and derivation that undoubtedly remain are all mine.

Contributors: Mary Allen, Dave Austin, Nick Austin, Alistair Beaton, Margaret Benton, Nick and Mary Butler, Alison Cathie, David Charters, Richard Clarke, Mike Coley-Smith, Lincoln Crawford, Michelle Doughty, Michael Fitzmaurice, Graham Forbes, Charles Frater, Phil Green, Steve Green, Yoz Graham, Gwyn Headley, Juliette Healey, Chris Holifield, John and Carol Kellas, Scott Kuhagen, Norman Lebrecht, Brian Levy, Shahjahan Madampat, Dirk Maggs, Strat Mastoris, Robert Moore, Tim Murari, Sushila Ravindranath, Pete and Pat Ridpath, David Sells, Alison Skilbeck, Howard Smith, Bryan Stevens, Brad Thompson, Catherine Webb, Eve Webb, Sue Webb, Sadie Wickham, Alan Williams, Shirley Williams.

Phil Green produced the admirably clear graphics in Part Three: Crapmatics. Thanks are due to my editors, Jane Donovan and Steve Gove, who were helpful and painstaking beyond the call of duty.

Bruce Robertson and Jim Williams entered into the spirit of the exercise and deserve special thanks not only for sending me many fine examples but also for their encouragement. Alistair Beaton read the final typescript and gave invaluable editorial advice for which I am deeply grateful.

Sir Winston Churchill famously remarked that Britain and America are divided by a common tongue. Certainly there are many nuances, allusions, and figures of speech that do not travel well across the Atlantic in either direction. For that reason, I would like particularly to thank the editor of the U.S. edition, Aaron Schlechter, for his exemplary editorial care and for his creativity in finding examples and references for American readers.

Finally, my thanks to Sue Webb for putting up with me while I was writing this book. During that time we would frequently interrupt each other in mid-sentence with the sudden cry of an unrelated word for possible inclusion in the dictionary. To an observer we must have looked borderline insane.

Introduction

Introduction to the American Edition, and Some Theories of Bullshit

There is a story told of three publishers at the Frankfurt Book Fair—a German, a Frenchman, and an American. They are having dinner together on expenses (which, during the Fair, is the only way). Now on their third bottle of Brunello, they are feeling discursive.

"*Ach, mein Gott*," says Hans to his American pal. "Bill, I am just so—*wie sagt man auf Englisch?*—so pissed with all the rubbish we translate from English into German. *Ich habe die Nase voll*, as we say here. All that dreck. Why is it that the traffic is so one-way? Not only do we have great literature of our own, but it so happens that German is the best language in the world."

"Hans," says Bill, "I grant you a certain Yankee cultural imperialism, but German the best language? Give me a break."

"No, no," says Hans. "For clarity German beats all others. The adjectives have endings so there is no messing about. We know the nouns they qualify. The adverbs obey word order rules so we understand exactly what they mean. The verbs stack up neatly at the end of the sentence, every one of which is engineered with the exactness—is that the word?—of an S-class Mercedes Benz. This is the reason German was for centuries the language of science and philosophy. Wittgenstein's great *Tractatus* could only have been written in German. And all those sibilant sounds…There is nothing so elegant as the German of Schiller, Heine, or Goethe. Think of the passion and precision of Rilke. It is the folly of history that has given your frightful language such pre-eminence. There can be no doubt that German is the best."

At this moment Pierre, a superbly dressed Parisian, overcomes his languor. "*Je m'em fou*," he says. "I care little for this debate, but as a matter of *verité*, it happens that French is supreme. No other language is as sexy and subtle. Of course it is often ambiguous, it is true. That is why French is the language of diplomacy—but in that ambiguity there is, I think, some 'ope for mankind. And as for elegance—*dis donc*, the Alexandrine in the hands of Racine or Corneille…Such beauty. It is divine, a marriage of form and sensuality that German with its *achtung! achtung!* sore throat and English with its—how do you say?—plum up the mouth can never equal. Even the football results have romance. Can you not 'ear the rustle of silken panties every time? For," observes Pierre with an urbane smile, "is not French also the language of love?"

Now the American publisher is getting a little irritated with all this clever-clogs European name-dropping. Racine, Wittgenstein. Enough. As he struggles to devise a rejoinder that will silence his friends, he finds himself casting about the table for inspiration.

"Look," he says, picking up a knife, "Hans, correct me if you will. Is this not what you Germans would call *ein Messer*?"

"*Bestimmt*," says Hans, "that is *ein Messer*."

"And Pierre," says the American, "in French I think it is a *couteau.*"

"*Absolument*," nods Pierre.

"But in English we call it a knife. And, guys, let's face it. *That's what it is.*"

Variations of this joke are told with differing degrees of resentment all over the world, for on our planet, the most useful language happens to be English. This is not a matter of the size of the Anglophone world. Mandarin Chinese (900 million), Hindi (380 million), and Spanish (360 million) all have larger communities of native speakers, though English is by far the most frequently studied second language. It has become the international language for business, entertainment, and technology, and its ascendancy—to the dismay of some language partisans like the French—is now so overwhelming that it cannot be challenged. Spread globally in the age of empire by the British, it was left behind as the least ignoble aspect of a dodgy colonial heritage (India, for instance, has more English speakers than the UK). In the twentieth century the rise of English took on an inexorable momentum. The reason, of course, was that it is the language of the dominant culture of the developed world, the United States of America, a linguistic as well as commercial and military superpower.

American English gave the old mother tongue a welcome injection of vitality. Waves of immigration into the United States brought with it rhythms, wit, figures of speech, grammatical constructions, and new words from many sources. In 1918 Theodore Roosevelt asserted robustly that if immigrants to the America had not learned English within five years of their arrival, they should be thrown out.

Promiscuously absorbing, translating, and adapting from every other language, spoken and written English now boasts the biggest lexicon on earth—as anybody can confirm who has risked a hernia by attempting to lift the twenty huge volumes (including supplement) of the *Complete Oxford English Dictionary*. And yet, if you attune yourself to the subtleties, in many parts of the States you can still hear still hear the fossil remains of other tongues like Italian, German, Polish, or Swedish.

One common usage has even borrowed a word order rule from another language. Only a few decades ago *hopefully* meant full of hope. Now it has become an all-purpose word placed at the beginning of a sentence to indicate that the proposition that follows is vaguely desirable. This verbal asylum seeker snuck into America via *hoffentlich* in German, which has another word for full of hope (*hoffnungsvoll*). Interestingly, in German *hoffentlich* always starts the sentence, a grammatical convention that we

English speakers have taken over without knowing its provenance. If you think about it, *hopefully* reverts to its original meaning when it appears in a sentence other than as the first word. "How do you see the future? Hopefully hopefully…"

The rolling cadences of Garrison Keillor, for example, are quite Scandinavian. Creole contains much French along with other borrowings, and in New York you would need a tin ear not to notice the influence of Yiddish. The latter has given English an appealing vocabulary (nosh, schlep, chutzpah…) that sometimes, like some transplanted bloom, pops up unexpectedly in conversation thousands of miles from its traditional communities.

American English has fantastic vitality and inventiveness, and, like all languages, it is evolving and changing. There is no point in trying, like the Académie in France, to ossify a "pure" version that is somehow said to embody the finest expression of the culture. America has a fine complement of acerbic grammarians such as William Safire or Edwin Newman (in some ways the great H.L. Mencken was the grand daddy of them all) who write witty if melancholy articles mourning the passing of the subjunctive or noting the loss of some subtle distinction. Their efforts are but a pebble tossed into a river of change, and their grief carries no sanction. America has no linguistic policemen whipping out their dictionaries as they handcuff some miscreant. ("Hey, buddy, what do you think you're playing at putting a nice word like this in a sentence like that? You're under arrest. You have the right to remain silent—and I advise you to do so…")

Linguistic evolution is unstoppable. What's more, it is blindingly swift and global. Instant communication, the simultaneous release of films to the international market (in part to reduce piracy), international travel, and the feverish business that is the sale of TV programming all conspire to help local slang or some scriptwriter's witty turn of phrase to replicate all over the world like a virus. The words of a Californian Valley Girl trying on a top in the Gap will be on the lips of a teenager in London within weeks. New coinages become ubiquitous at astonishing speed. The lexicographers of the *OED* cannot find a reference to "pear-shaped" prior to 1973 that has to do with anything other than fruit.

Language will always be shifting because it is used by human beings—an endlessly creative and capricious lot who, despite possessing, according to Chomsky and other theorists, an innate talent for verbal pattern making, are largely indifferent to the more persnickety rules of grammar. Language is our most extraordinary achievement. It differentiates us from the animals and forms the basis of all civilization, for without it the transmission of knowledge and such cooperative endeavors as agriculture would have been impossible. What are consciousness and thought without language to give them form?

Unfortunately language is not only mankind's greatest invention; it is also the vessel of an astonishing pitch and volume of bullshit. We humans have a genius for waffle, trickery, self-deception, euphemism, and every kind of verbally camouflaged dishonesty.

So what is bullshit? And how can we distinguish it from lying? The key difference is that in order to lie, we must first know the truth. Then—as a conscious act of volition—we may find it in our mendacious little hearts to dissemble. Bullshit, on the other hand, is built into the very language we use. We may choose bullshitty words in order to fib, but the greater danger is that a bullshit-laden vocabulary has percolated so deeply into our thought processes that we can no longer recognize it for what it is. The bullshitter deceives himself as well as others.

This brings us to the definition of bullshit and also a theory. To keep this book to a manageable length, there have to be some limiting criteria. Jargon is a kind of technical slang between members of a group with shared enthusiasms or esoteric knowledge. It is often bullshitty in intention, for it does not exist just to enable information to be exchanged with maximum economy between buffs, but also to dress up technicalities as more arcane than they merit and, more importantly, exclude outsiders. Slang and patois are similar inasmuch as they define a community of users and exclude others. But bullshit is much broader; it permeates our intellectual processes.

Bullshit comes in many varieties. Some are so transparent that we merely sigh. Much advertising hyperbole falls into this category. "Classic" T-shirts, "groundbreaking" bottle-openers—we may want to be spared such claims, but we are unlikely to do more than wince a little. When a realtor describes an apartment as "intimate," we grin because we know it is a code word for a room so small that there can be no sex unless somebody is prepared to stick a limb out of the window. This is just bullshit with a lowercase b. There's lots of this, much of it amusing and relatively harmless—and usually comprising everyday words only rendered bullshitty by their absurd context. (These small units of bullshit have been named "coproemes"—a useful term for which I must thank the writer and lawyer Jim Williams.)

Bullshit with a capital B is more dangerous, for it describes words and phrases informed by a worldview that may not be understood by the user. Capital B Bullshit is weapons grade. It is ingrained so deeply that it affects the speaker's ability to think clearly. That lack of focus is part of the seduction; we don't always want the light of unforgiving clarity to shine upon our actions. Bullshit casts a deep shadow.

Military language is the best-known example of this attempt to blind oneself from the reality and consequences of one's actions. "Collateral damage," for instance, has long been seen as a sickening euphemism. More recently "extraordinary rendition," "waterboarding," or "enhanced interrogation techniques" all condense a cloud of verbal fog over torture.

Those using these ugly and devalued expressions are not necessarily wicked. They could well be honest people who have been desensitized by the relentless use of such terminology or—at worst—completely insulated by it from the reality of what they are describing. Not only does "enhanced interrogation technique" sound better than torture, the phrase allows somebody to *think* it without all the connotations of agony and cruelty that would be evoked by the more old-fashioned term.

Something similar may happen in other organizations with a strong sense of hierarchy and pressure to conform to a collective goal. Corrupt corporations, for instance, are not inhabited only by villains, yet the circumscribed language that is the norm in many big companies makes it more difficult for those who have a feeling that something is amiss to find the words to express their unease. "Problem" is almost taboo; instead there are situations, opportunities, issues, and challenges—words that are not only evasive but almost always used in a collective context. The "issues" are the property of all—not the individual. Bullshit is the essential language of group thinking.

This is the point about Bullshit. Bullshit diffuses personal responsibility. Over the years its moral content has leaked away like air from a slow puncture. When Michael Douglas described himself as having a sex "addiction," he ceased to be fecklessly promiscuous. The poor chap became the victim of a medical—rather than a moral—condition.

Of course our appetite for lying to ourselves seems to be built into human nature and is not a unique characteristic of English. Every language on earth lends itself to it. Japanese, for example, is stunningly good at passive constructions. The verb *naru*—to become—is often deployed in this context. A Japanese manager will not say, "I have decided…" Instead he will note that "it has *become* necessary…" (to let you all go, perhaps).

German has a genius for distancing itself from the immediate by flight into abstraction; nearly every adjective, for instance, can be turned into a noun by the addition of a suffix (...*lichkeit*...*einkeit*). Arabic has a multitude of fatalistic ways of saying that Allah wills it, so it cannot be the fault of the individual. Some philosophical concepts sound vastly more engaging in French even though they turn out to be Bullshit after a moment's thought.

But despite the ubiquity of the phenomenon, English, and American English in particular, are great mother lodes of toxic Bullshit, and by its very dominance the United States leads the field.

Doubtless, it is impudent for a foreigner to speculate about why this should be, but with some temerity I would like—with apologies in advance for generalizing too glibly—to suggest some reasons.

Firstly, the American genius for Bullshit reflects a paradox at the heart of American society—for Bullshit thrives on contradiction. There is surely no other country on Earth that tells itself such a positive story about its place in the world. (Of course it is absurd to personify a vast and diverse country, so please take the caveats as read.) Britons know that we have a long history—inter alia—of degenerate monarchs, fearsome snobbery, bellicose colonialism, and grim mistreatment of our workers. America, on the other hand, thinks of itself as a good guy—the country with the white hat. The history of the extermination, more or less, of its original inhabitants was sanitized into myth even as it happened. There's even an American dream. (Who would talk of the Belgian dream, or the Romanian dream, without a smile?) But human nature does not change with geography. Americans are as fallible as the rest of us. It is the tension between the American desire to "tell it like it is" and actually how it is that has generated so much Bullshit—especially in politics, business, and the military.

Just like the imperial powers of history, the U.S. is pursuing its interests around the world with the finesse of a hand grenade. With a sleight of hand akin to the way the nineteenth-century Brits exploited the planet under the guise of bringing civilization to the dusky natives, American foreign policy talks about police actions, sanctions, the domino effect, international law, peacekeeping operations, the Monroe doctrine, and maintaining spheres of influence—all of which are invoked to justify "interventions," often of a military nature, in the name of liberty. Some of these overseas excursions are genuinely generous. Others are not, and the hurt and bewilderment of the American public when the locals resist are all the more poignant because the language drafted in to cover these adventures wears the cloak of nobility.

American corporations offer another rich seam for lexicographers chipping away in the Bullshit mine. The USA is a huge country. Its very scale has a romance of the bleak for someone from a somewhere small. (A British road movie, for instance, even with a soundtrack of Bob Dylan singing rambling-on songs through his nose, is risible.) On average an American will move houses seventeen times in a lifetime, three times as often as a European. The population is restive and is imbued with the idea that work is hard and that to get on, you must get up off your backside and hustle. Despite—or probably because of—this, American corporations place extraordinary value on belonging. ("We value teamwork here; we all gotta sing from the same hymn sheet.") The pressure to "share the values" is intense; mavericks may be sidelined. TV series portray the office as a haven of good-natured joshing, flirtation, and warmth, almost a surrogate for the family life that eludes so many (and not just Americans). In organizations with this strong sense of ethos, the display of anything other than a breezy optimism and a conviction that the company comes first, right or wrong, may be construed as disloyalty.

And here lies another paradox: American business is ruthless. It always was. The nineteenth-century robber barons like Gould, Vanderbilt, and Astor (whose pursuit of self-interest helped to build the nation) would have regarded the reinvention of big companies as pillars of the community as purest humbug. Corporations are not only wily and predatory in their dealings with their competitors but also in their treatment of their own employees. Wall Street commentators will describe an executive as aggressive in the most complimentary tones, and the appointment of a flint-hearted toughie with a record of hacking away at the costs (usually the humans) will be rewarded with a fillip in the share price, something especially gratifying to those with share options. U.S. labor law, for example, offers little protection to the workers, many of whom suffer the anxiety of "no cause" termination clauses in their contracts of employment.

The dismal fact is that in many corporations, dear old Chuck and Biff, your neatly suited colleagues with an affable manner and those dazzling teeth that are the envy of the world, are trying to knife you between the shoulder blades. Far from frowning on this kind of behavior, CEOs may encourage it. Divide and rule is the old adage; besides, perhaps it keeps everybody sharp. This contradiction between the corporation as family and the corporation as the damn setting for feral in-fighting is hard to contemplate unflinchingly. Corporation-speak—with its human resources, rightsizing, relationship management, through-put efficiencies, overheads, and so on—avoids this unpalatable truth by using language entirely bleached of any hint of emotional or moral color.

Management theory, a largely American invention, has a similar function. Management is presented as a *science* or at least a technical discipline. Control that inventory, fine-tune the supply train, structure the line management efficiently, research the market, and you're laughing. How many management books say there is a moral dimension to the process? That if you treated people decently they might reciprocate?

Paradoxically, another aspect of American life, rightly seen as attractive, can lead to Bullshit. It's this: the U.S. is the most technologically advanced and innovative country on Earth; historically, its industrial and technical superiority has served it well. The best American universities are the best on the planet. Venture capitalists are constantly on the lookout for the smart MIT graduate equipped with a bright idea and the expectation of making a serious wad. The uniquely favorable American regulatory framework (in part courtesy of senators Bayh and Dole) gooses that ambition. In the great market free-for-all, anybody can succeed if he or she can come up with the equivalent of Emerson's better mousetrap. It's an integral part of the American dream, and it is predicated on a very potent idea, one held in almost superstitious awe: every problem must have a solution.

The Bullshit arises when this appealing notion is allowed to ooze beyond the technical. Yankee know-how will prevail—even in those messy corners of life in which competence is hard to define. The pressure for success is relentless. An American must succeed not just in business, but also as a lover, a parent, a dieter, a spiritually fulfilled being, a healthy person, an investor, and in many other roles—for as an American you are entitled to the best life has to offer. Naturally, for every vexation there will be an answer—preferably one embodied in a paperback costing not more than $9.95. Twelve steps, three rules, seven habits, thirty seconds, EQ, bell curves, S-curves, five minutes a day, F plans, GI indices—the huge American self-help industry, the biggest on the planet both in volume and pro rata, reads with the matter-of-factness of a manual for self-assembly furniture. Fundamentally, it seems to be saying, we are all okay. If we are still assailed by grief and frailty, there can only be some pesky technical glitch (poor communication perhaps) that will soon be fixed. The human condition, in all its ambiguity, joy, and insoluble tragedy, is medicalized and reduced to bullet points. Just follow these instructions, and you will be once again on the sunlit uplands.

This profound fib generates huge quantities of Bullshit and surely is the source of much unhappiness. Some problems do not admit of solution, but unimaginable quantities of Bullshit are consumed in the belief that they are. Religious certainty and New Age mysticism also furnish means of not contemplating the human condition without blinking, and in these respects too, America—though not alone—is one of the world leaders.

No matter how suspect our intentions, language can dress them in noble finery. However depraved in fact, a speaker with a good script can be disguised with a sympathetic voice and spurious authority. In that regard, we should listen out for words, especially technical ones, appropriated from other contexts. When a politician uses the term "parameters" instead of "limits," she is misleadingly borrowing a precision from another discipline. We must never forget that a fancy vocabulary is the dazzle camouflage of Bullshit.

The fluent have always exercised power over the inarticulate. Even George Washington had help with his oratory from Alexander Hamilton. The growth of radio and then television, which happened first in the U.S., enabled politicians to reach over the heads of well-informed local critics to a national audience. It is no accident that, with the scurrilous exception of Dr. Goebbels, American movers and shakers woke up to the power of the media before the rest of the world. American presidents employ the most talented wordsmiths; the brightest graduates compete for an internship in the White House's Office of Speechwriting. President Reagan, for instance, went to some trouble to avoid sounding like "a pointy-headed intellectual" and, thanks largely to Peggy Noonan, his supremely gifted speechwriter, managed to sound lovably twinkly most of the time. Would President Kennedy's inauguration speech have lived on if Theodore Sorensen had not written it so well? Just occasionally, however, the linguistic conditioning goes awry. President Bush has practiced his own down-home persona so rigorously that in his anguish after 9/11, he fell back on the word "folks" to describe the Al-Qaeda attackers—a jarringly false note.

So all this is not mere pedantry. Aside from a few grammarians meeting secretly in seedy bars, we don't desperately care if people say "we're doing pretty good" as opposed to "we're doing pretty well." Will legions of men in tweed jackets with elbow patches march on Washington carrying carefully worded placards? "Save our adverbs! Now, please." Grammar is formalized from usage and is helpful to the extent that it aids clarity of meaning and the ease of reading or listening. But language itself can be beautiful, vivid, and comprehensible even with a quasi-criminal disregard of the rules.

No. It's not about elegance or nitpicking niceties. The vital point is that Bullshit lies at the very heart of executive power. At the beginning of his great novel *1984*, George Orwell quotes a slogan: "War is peace. Freedom is slavery. Ignorance is strength." He is telling us that if you can control the language, you control the means with which we think about the world.

This book is dedicated to all those who wish to keep their Bullshit detectors in combat trim.

PART ONE

Corporate Bullshit:
Let Me Share This with You

Corporation: an ingenious device for obtaining individual profit without individual responsibility.

—Ambrose Bierce, *The Devil's Dictionary*

Big businesses were built by men well-endowed with ego and energy who were not noticeably inhibited by scruple. Cornelius Vanderbilt, the great robber baron of the railways, did not build his empire without dirty tricks. Capital was a weapon. Rivals were bought out or ruined. The workforce did what it was told; unions were repressed, and intimidation from mercenaries broke strikes. Robber barons ended many of the great nineteenth-century labor disputes by employing armed Pinkertons, the private detective agency that played such an ignoble role in intimidation and strike breaking.

For the British worker, conditions were unspeakable. Overseas, there was even more license for employers. Before its power was finally handed over to the Crown, the British East India Company employed its own army. As recently as the mid nineteenth century, the Opium Wars forced the Chinese to grant trading rights by addicting their market to a dangerous product. Money, power, and ambition drove these enterprises, and heaven help those who stood in their path.

The point is this: business has always been run by competitive killers. It's a process whereby you make your product as cheaply as you can and sell it for the very maximum the market will bear.

Although the great personal fiefdoms have, with some exceptions, been replaced by corporations, they or their successors still attract people with the same motivation as their nineteenth-century forebears. In a process rather akin to Queen Victoria's reinvention of royalty as the ideal family (a role at which the inmates struggle pitiably), in modern times corporations have tried to redefine themselves as pillars of the establishment—and thus deeply respectable. Foundations, sponsorship (of the right sort), concert halls covered in logos, and beautifully produced statements of "values and vision" abound.

This PR polish notwithstanding, those at the top are uninhibited by shame. The ratio between the lowest wage and the highest has steadily increased to the point that it is possible for a CEO to be earning a thousand times more than a junior in the same corporation. In the last few decades, globalization has given corporations new opportunities for nifty footwork. Profits can be moved into low-tax economies; inter-company accounting allows the corporation to sell stuff to itself to boost turnover in key markets; and manufacturing flows across the world to whomever provides the cheapest and most desperate workforce.

Competition within and between corporations is feral, yet the language of corporations is reassuringly bland with a strong leaning towards the obscure, Latinate, and defensive. It is this disparity between the pretensions of corporate life and its savage reality that produces such a rich mother lode of Bullshit.

---

aggressive (adj.) Many corporations see this as a term of praise. Business is competitive, and to pretend otherwise is to indulge in self-deception. You need some predators out there being ruthless on your behalf. That's the thinking. It may hold some melancholy truth. But employers who pride themselves on their aggression direct much of it inwards so that such companies, riven with dread and footwork, will be hell to work for. An organization inhabited by amoral killers is likely to be debilitated by gnawing on its own entrails.

algorithm (n.) Borrowed from mathematics, the term describes a procedure or set of rules for a calculation designed to derive a particular sort of solution. Someone saying, "We'll devise an algorithm to address this" is being tautologous. It's rather like saying, "We'll invent problem-solving procedures to solve this problem."

bottom line (np.) Taken from accounting, in which the bottom line conventionally shows the profit (or loss), this has come to mean "Let's skip the footling detail and go straight to the relevant." If someone says, "The bottom line is—I'm leaving you," you are probably better off without him or her.

BPO (acronym) Business Process Outsourcing. See **outsourcing**.

brand (n.) Once upon a time, this was just a trademark or identifying label like the mark burnt on to cattle (etymologically *brand* and *burn* are siblings). Now brand management has become one of the buzz concepts of twenty-first-century commerce. The marketing, the design, the history, the social connotations, the position in the market—occasionally even the quality of the product itself—are all aspects of the brand. There's an inexplicit assumption behind the investment in branding: you have to sell the image when there's little to distinguish the product from its competitors. For instance, cigarettes are all very similar beneath the packaging (as the tar ratings show, numbers by definition allow ranking; in fact, the range between highest and lowest is not great). Toothpaste is a variation on the theme of titanium dioxide in a gel full of fresh-tasting chemicals and preservatives to ensure the shelf life of the product. Most quartz watches, regardless of the manufacturer, contain a movement made by Seiko.

Cosmetics are the direst example. Lipstick consists of a tube of purified animal or petroleum fat with some non-allergenic pigment in it. The unit cost is a few cents. The pretty cylinder with its up-and-down helical gear is more expensive, but still only cents. All the rest of the price is packaging, retailer's discount, profit and—to an extent unprecedented in any other product—the cost of branding. The trick of the brand managers is to persuade women that one tube of colored fat does wonders for their *amour propre* while another, chromatically and chemically identical but costing a tenth as much, makes them look cheap.

Absurdly, hard-eyed young men and women with careful haircuts and implausible teeth have taken to advertising themselves to head-hunters as brands.

buy in (v.) You "buy in" to a proposition. An executive might say, "Yep, I'll buy that," meaning that it's a credible idea. See also **sign up to**. Both usages suggest that believing is a commercial transaction in which the truth of the proposition is only one factor in its salability.

challenge (n.), **challenging** (adj.) Difficult. An "opportunity" is slightly less threatening than a "challenge." Both may be "issues," but neither is a **problem**.

comfortable (adj.) In cliff-face office blocks, this pleasant word is seldom applied to shoes, but frequently to decisions. "I'm comfortable with that" means yes. "Kind of uncomfortable" may suggest hard-to-calculate complexities. The expression is also used when the decision in question is morally dodgy. The subtext is that the speaker is a grown-up, burdened with knowledge about the ways of the world, and that at some personal cost, he can overcome his scruples. Instead of "uncomfortable," imagine saying, "It's wrong, but let's do it anyway." Much corporate language obscures any moral content, a technique perfected by the military with such infamous obscenities as "collateral damage."

consultants (n.) The consummate professionals of our time. They don't make anything—they just take a view. Consultants are bright and may have a lot to offer because of the catholic range of their experience. It can make sense to use them to deal with some one-off upheaval requiring staff with specialist skills whom it would not be economic to recruit permanently. Unfortunately directors, lacking both confidence and moral courage, tend to draft in consultants when they need a third party to blame for something unpalatable. Consultants are staggeringly expensive, partly because they have perfected the art of teasing out the bleeding obvious and partly because their clients are so inept at specifying the task in the first place. See also **consultancies** under Political Bullshit.

core competency (n./jargon) Gurus of management theory maintain that it is a science. It has no moral content; it's just a matter of moving the components around into the best configuration. According to this thinking, there is often some basic skill—or competency—at which the company excels (selling copyrights, making steel...). Everything else is peripheral, and thus can be given less attention or contracted out to third parties. This notion has led to the fragmentation of once well-integrated businesses.

core values (n./jargon) This is flattering, for it presupposes that the corporation has values.

customers (n.) A decent word and usually bullshit free, but in some contexts it can be compromised. On America's trains and subways, the traveling public no longer consists of passengers but of customers. Now that many utilities are privatized, the word may be precise; it also tells us something about the disappearance of a social contract between these organizations and the public. You are not the beneficiary of an ethos of social obligation. You're a customer.

data mining (v.) Clever analytic techniques exercised by expensive IT gurus may reveal something about your complicated business that would otherwise not be obvious. You just see the headline figures (widget sales up—yippee). But digging reveals that all your extra widgets are being channeled through a K-Mart in Wichita for a project due to close on Thursday. Opening a new plant would therefore be daft. But do you believe that the organization does not know this already?

Why is data mining necessary in the first place? There's a saying that a printout ten inches thick is data, but a printout of two pages is information. Your IT system should give you the latter. Be wary of IT. It's there to serve you—not vice versa. It holds a terrible fascination for a certain kind of person (usually male) who will explore its complexities in a state of palsied preoccupation. Unless you are running a software-development house, this is unhelpful.

downshifting (n. and v.) Jargon for an escape from the stresses of the big job and the horrors of office footwork to a smaller, less lucrative, but more pleasurable role. The most passionate advocates of downshifting are those who have given it all up to tend their own olive grove in Tuscany or vineyard in Napa. For such satisfying transformations, it is essential to have a cabbage-sized wad in the bank.

downsizing (n. and v.) Wholesale reduction in the size of the workforce and closure of plants (overseas if possible). "Downsizing" is a clever euphemism because it contains within itself a kind of rationale for what it is. It sounds as if it affects an entire industry, i.e., it's not merely a short-term expedient but a response to those uncontrollable global conditions. This may be the case, but the use of the word does not guarantee it.

drivers (n.) In business circles, always a plural. These are not men with tattoos and an 18-wheeler, but the vital factors determining whether your business is sustainable. "Drivers" are usually obvious things like sales, margins, and overhead expenses. Such old-fashioned terms do not sound so crisp.

flexible (adj.) In a fast-changing world, this is a desirable quality in a workforce. However, we should not confuse it with docile, abject, or browbeaten. If you have been employed as a postgraduate geneticist, but the company decides to redeploy you as a fork-lift driver in their warehouse in Oshkosh, Wisconsin, you should be grateful for the opportunity to demonstrate your flexibility.

The word is also used by politicians. They invoke it when they are opposing or sweeping away legislation designed to protect the working stiff on the grounds that somewhere in the world, somebody is prepared to undertake the same task for a wage almost imperceptible by the human eye. See also **red tape**.

GAAS (CPA's acronym for Generally Accepted Auditing Standards)
Spare a thought for America's certified public accountants. They are often accused of having a spreadsheet where their hearts ought to be or of living with their mothers for too long after qualifying. In fact, they do a difficult job balancing the interests of the state with those of their clients, many of whom will duck and weave in order to bend the rules. Cloddish hints that next year the client might find a more amenable accountant are drearily familiar to any CPA who has been in practice for more than ten minutes.

This book is far too short to begin to describe the complexity of GAAS. There are tens of thousands of pages of regulation covering everything from the meaning of fair value to having lunch on expenses. Every year, huge books (never less than 800 pages and $75) are published that outline the latest updates to auditing practice. Professional CPAs are obliged to keep current with a library of new publications, digests, and advice. They hardly have time for human relations.

GAAS tries to define every contingency and legislate for it. This represents an astonishing accumulation of detail and a breath-taking investment of intellectual effort. That is why GAAS documentation has grown so huge and elaborate—and also why it merits inclusion in a book on bullshit.

The attempt to cover everything, the whole works, brings out a terrible ingenuity in those of a larcenous bent. What a challenge. If it's not specifically against the rules in GAAS, then it must be legal. Right?

The other approach—not without its own risks—would be to have a system based on principles. Accountants are usually pretty bright, and it is surprisingly difficult for one to pretend not to have understood the applicable principle.

Pitting your wits against GAAS is a game that has served corporate America well. But is it such good news for the public?

game plan (n.) What's so feeble about a mere plan? What is it with these sporting metaphors? Do they make the speakers feel more virile? Nobody has a mere plan these days; they even have a game plan for dinner. It's the same with records. It has to be a track record.

get with the program (v./threat) Do what you are told.

going forward (catchphrase) Business language is gung-ho. Anybody not sharing the vision would soon feel icy winds blowing up their pants. "Going forward" as in "we're looking at this investment going forward" does not describe an improving investment. No, it just means "in the future." But time does not merely pass at the usual rate in corporate circles. That would be too passive. Everything makes progress going forward.

good at admin (adj. phrase) Fortunately there are tidy-minded people around who just get on with the work. But there is also a strange notion that being good at admin is such a virtue that it does not matter if you have any knowledge of the formal content of the organization. Let's appoint this person to run our nuclear power station because he was so deft at the detail in his doughnut business…Hence, "good at admin" managers— sometimes at the CEO level—can parachute into companies about whose business they have almost immaculate ignorance. It may take a year or two before they leave with a large payoff and a dying company in their wake.

granularity (n.) This technical word has acquired a genuinely mystifying dimension of bullshit. "Granularity" in reports seems to be about detail. Perhaps it is an antidote to generalization. Maybe the lack of it is techie code for "lazy."

hopefully (adv.) Via German (*hoffentlich*), this word, when it appears at the beginning of a sentence, is now almost universally accepted as qualifying the proposition that follows. "Hopefully" in the sense of full of hope, with high morale, recovers its old meaning in other positions in the sentence, just as it does if you knock off the adverbial suffix -*ly* and turn the word back into an adjective. In business circles the new model word is "irresistible," for it fulfills that vital function of much business and political language: it avoids responsibility. "Hopefully [what follows will be the case]" does not commit the speaker in the same way as "I hope that…," "I expect…," or, God forbid, "I promise…"

hot desking (jargon) You are expected to be out in the field (Field? Pittsburgh on a rainy Thursday in January?), ducking and weaving on the company's behalf. When you do venture into HQ, you haven't a desk or a chair to call your own. You may share a "work station." Sounds inviting, doesn't it? Is it any wonder that you feel semi-detached?

Human Resources (oxymoron) As oxymoronic indeed as "fun run." Companies with HR departments invariably say how much they cherish their workers, in whose skills they readily invest. However, they are undermined by an irony deficit. HR is one of those **MBA** management terms which sounds good, but betrays itself. The word "resources" makes no distinction between people and bits of machinery to be moved about at will. The "Personnel Department" was more honest, obviously being part of the management structure and not pretending to be cuddly.

illegal operation (np.) This has nothing to do with the directors setting up a pension fund in the Cayman Islands. It's a screen message that pops up whenever you try to get your computer to do what you want without following with obsessive literal-mindedness a needlessly long and counter-intuitive procedure. You will be punished. It will send your credit card details to Lagos, write a rude letter to your bank, and rat on you to the IT manager who will then patronize you unendurably while putting it right.

interface (n. and v.) Where man and computer meet. For goodness sake, unless you're joking, you don't "interface" with your partner. You can't reboot your wife or husband when you've ruined the most important relationship in your life…

just in time… (adv. phrase) This revolution in inventory management, originally from Japan, transformed the car industry and many other manufacturing processes. Though complex enough to have spawned suites of specialist software, supplying "just in time" is undeniably rational. It means that a company no longer holds stock of vital components that would tie up space and, more importantly, money, but arranges for their delivery so that they arrive just in time for use. The thinking behind "just in time" has spread across the land and become orthodoxy—and thus dangerous. In some industries—publishing, for example—the rate of sale is hard to predict. The lack of availability of a title—even for a few days—might well encourage a potential buyer to go for another book actually on the shelf.

In the War in Iraq, just-in-time stock control claimed a blood sacrifice when the armor needed by soldiers was still "downstream" in the supply train; the people shooting at these troops were no respecters of management theory. The technique works well if applied to continuous processes with a smooth pattern of demand, but it does not cope with the unexpected. Nobody is prepared to hold a strategic reserve anymore (not even of such frivolities as a vaccine for the potentially pandemic avian flu) when the money could be put to other uses.

knowledge management (np.) Fancy filing; lots of meetings.

KPIs (acronym) Key Performance Indicators. KPIs were invented in order to quantify the unquantifiable. That is why they are especially popular in social services and local government. KPIs are seized upon by managers who are unsure of their own judgment or who inhabit organizations so twitchy that they feel the need to put such assessments on an "objective" basis in case of subsequent litigation.

lean and mean (adjectival corporate cliché) Does this suggest that a company is honed by the operation of Darwinian processes to a point where it is as efficient as a freshly unwrapped razor blade? Or does it mean understaffed and horrible? See also **aggressive**.

legacy (n.) Disparaging term applied to existing and perfectly functional IT systems by those hoping to sell you something more sophisticated. The implementation of the new system will push your business to the brink.

let go (v.) To fire from a job. This term is now so universal that many people don't see it as a euphemism. But it was once meant to imply that the boss would only with a poor grace let someone of such stellar quality escape from his employ. Recently "dehiring" has made an appearance. See also **outplacement**.

The compassion or otherwise with which people get fired provides an insight into a company's values. For example, in the testosterone-drenched corporation run by Robert Maxwell, there was a perverse pride in behaving badly because it showed you had the toughness needed to be a "player." There the synonym for firing was "killing."

leverage (n. and v.) Aristotle said that with a lever long enough, he could move the world. "Leverage" entered financial jargon in the 1980s. "Leveraging one's assets" was a phrase never far from the lips of men with icy spreadsheets where their hearts ought to be. The idea seems clear enough—that somehow you get your assets to work harder by using them to gain influence or exercise power. But how exactly? Putting them up for sale? Presumably you are making the most of them already. A recent sighting of the word in an advertisement for Compaq computers boasted of "leveraging a color palate."

logistics (n.) A term borrowed from the military. You take delivery of your products, keep an eye on how many you've got and where you've put them, and ship them out again to suitably invoiced customers. This used to happen in mere warehouses, but now gleaming logistics centers add some mystery to the process.

low-hanging fruit (n.) An odd expression for some easily achieved aim. It's not bullshit exactly, but it does have a strangely moist and Old Testament feel. Managers, as do we all, find the little tasks more tractable than the whoppers. Rather than ignoring the big

problems (opportunities), they might, with the help of this fruity metaphor, dress up their grasp of the trivial as a policy decision.

management retreat (np.) This is not what it sounds. Companies seeking to **re-engineer** their business might take the management team off to some island, usually a traffic island with a hotel on it. There, away from the press of everyday panics, the managers will be able to think **outside the box**. Such off-site meetings are excruciating. They quickly revert to business as usual—footwork, politics, currying favor, shafting colleagues, and so on.

Even more painful are "team-building exercises" involving paintball guns or constructing a bridge over a torrent with only a plank, a piece of string, and an empty beer can. Frustrated soldiers and borderline psychos do well in such exercises.

meta- (pretentious prefix) Borrowed from philosophy; meta-language, for instance, is language about language. In corporate circles, meta-data is data about data. Statistics about how well your software is performing might be described as meta-data by **MBAs** in crisp shirts and glittery glasses. Everyday language would do, but then the mysteries would not be protected. See also **data mining**.

mission (n.) Often found conjoined, as in "mission statement," this word is another queasy attempt to suffuse the hard-nosed activity of money-making with a kind of religiosity.

Of course, business people should have some idea of where they are going and how their business fits into the wider picture, but they can usually express those ideas in a sentence or two. "The demand for pixel processors will remain high, reflecting the economy's shift towards image-intensive digital industries. We pixel-processor manufacturers will not only stay in business, but grow. We've decided not to diversify into computer game development. We hope to improve our margins and overtake Megacorp as the number one in North America. P.S. Will be humane to the staff and keep a beady eye on any relevant new technology…" The trick is to expand these pieties (for business plans tend not to survive their first encounter with markets) into pages and pages of impressive prose. In keeping with the evangelical flavor of the language, mission statements are often suffused with a cringe-making revivalist optimism. See also **vision**.

[go] off-line (adj. and v.) Off the record, outside the usual framework, or hanging up…Computer metaphors rule. "I've got a window, so I'm going off-line to interact with the kids…" See also **interface**.

off shoring (n.) See **outsourcing**.

on-the-job training (np.) Throw them in and see if they drown.

outcome focused (jargon) Well, who isn't?

outcome indicators (jargon) Did we succeed? Better check the outcome indicators. See **outcome focused**.

outplacement (n.) Firing senior staff. The company hires a specialist counseling firm to advise redundant executives. As a result, outplacement has evolved into a euphemistic verb (to outplace). The U.S. government has also come up with expressions like "RIF" (reduction in force) and "Personnel Ceiling Reductions."

outside the box (catchphrase) Radical, innovative—an invention of the management books of the 1980s. There is a large publishing industry devoted to management theory, none of which has any moral content. Many titles boast neat illustrations with schematic humans and Venn diagrams. Teamwork will overlap with strategy, perhaps, and the shaded area will represent the target. This is of incalculable help in the office. Boxes abound, and some are connected with thick arrows and some with dotted lines. Of course there are many helpful ideas in these books—but there are also Alps of Bullshit.

Recently, management gurus have become embarrassed by the clichéd nature of the box and have invented "helicopter thinking." "Blue skies thinking" is also popular among those with a more lyrical bent. Both expressions flatter the user that his or her imagination is not earthbound. See also **silo mentality**.

The reason that ideas are outside the box in the first place is that most of them are crap.

outsourcing (n. and v.) In the 1980s, management theorists came up with the idea that companies had a "core business" and that the other bits and pieces common to all businesses could be bought in from contractors. It makes sense if you are a small company unable to afford the first-rate technical services you need in order to compete with giants. For example, distribution benefits from economies of scale, so why not buy that service from a specialist company big enough to afford the latest technology? But outsourcing is not axiomatically right in all areas. Do you want your bills paid by third parties who have no knowledge of your business? See also **logistics**.

Once applicable to such functions as IT, building maintenance, financial services, and so on, the idea has expanded to embrace the wholesale manufacture of a company's goods in low labor-cost economies. This now global practice is called **off shoring**. In an age when telecommunications are cheap, international firms in the West now even find it profitable to ship out data processing.

Every firm outsourcing manufacture to China or IT to India is driven by expediency, but the aggregate effect of all those individual decisions will be huge. For places like Bangalore, with its well-educated Anglophone workforce, the result is an influx of wealth, but from a system point of view, you might think that there's a risk of impoverishing the markets for which the bulk of the cheaply produced goods and services are destined. Perhaps the decline of self-indulgent old economies and the rise of new ones are built in to the cyclical ups and downs of capitalism—if we live long enough to see it. Economists tell us not to worry. Apparently western societies are entering a post-industrial age in which there will be little manufacturing. People will work in service industries by exploiting the "value-added" end of the chain of supply, and the rest of the economy will somehow function by everybody taking in each other's laundry.

ownership (n.) Not of the company, of course, but of particular projects. Corporate structures tend to diffuse responsibility, so in order to restore it, the writers of management books have come up with this notion. In practice, it means stress rather than shares, anxiety not equity. See also **sign up to**.

paperless office (risible aspiration) Once upon a time, we believed that computers would reduce or even eliminate the need for paper. But, oddly, the printers got ever faster until now we have blindingly quick laser printers that can spew out reams of stuff in the time it takes to say "hard copy." Whole forests shudder whenever some new business software comes on to the market. Why? Technology versus human nature—a knockout in round one. We just don't trust electronic records yet. In the event of a wrangle about who said what to whom (and who cleared up afterwards), we feel that we are better covered with a tangible piece of paper in our hands.

paradigm (n.) In Thomas Kuhn's famous history of science, *The Structure of Scientific Revolutions*, a paradigm was a set of ideas and concepts representing the received wisdom of the day. In philosophy, a paradigm, or paradigm case, is an apt example or neat piece of reasoning so well chosen that it can be treated as exemplifying a general argument. But in management circles, the word means whatever you want it to mean.

passive (the voice in grammar rather than the adj.) Often found in political as well as management circles, the use of the passive is one of the many linguistic tricks for avoiding responsibility and aspiring to counterfeit gravitas. If somebody says, "It would seem that this [factory, perhaps] is inviable," the appropriate response is to ask to whom it would seem that way, and why. Similarly, a lazy journalist might write, "It has been reported today..." Where? An official press release? A pinch from another news agency? A taxi driver told him on the way from the airport?

British civil servants writing reports have been forbidden the use of the passive voice. They still hedge brilliantly, but at least their caveats and disclaimers are explicit. Entire press releases can be written in the passive, especially when the copywriter is trying to sound honest—but without actually naming anybody. See **mistakes** under Political Bullshit.

position (n. and v.) "I'm not in a position to…" means no. It's a good example of the diffusion of responsibility that so characterizes corporate language. Perhaps the executive genuinely suffers from limits of authority or interference from above. Perhaps not. This expression (imagine it in response to a request for a raise) implies that he or she would love to be helpful were it not for those frightful pressures and complexities that less senior people can scarcely comprehend. "The big picture" is another phrase often extracted from this armory.

Nouns frequently mutate into verbs. "Position"—as in "We've positioned the company…"—is usefully brief, though rather ugly. "Impact" as a verb is more wince-making. "Position" has another meaning in which it often stars as a bullshit conveyor. "My position [on some issue]…" sounds like it has been arrived at after much intellectual tussling with the pros and cons; clearly, it must be better thought out than a mere opinion.

power napping (v.) Executives have mastered this valuable technique and often cite Winston Churchill as its most talented exponent. Ordinary workers merely fall asleep on the job.

proactive (adj.) So much sexier than just doing something…

problem (n.) It's best to avoid this word, lest you be thought negative. **Challenge** is handy, though on no account smirk when you utter it.

productivity (n.) This is a "hurrah word" (see Political Bullshit, page 30), self-evidently a Good Thing. But it is worth remembering that it measures output per unit of labor. If demand is not growing, productivity can be increased by reducing the number of workers. It's an aspect of the **MBA** school of thinking whereby management enhances its pretense of being a science by replacing such notions as loyalty to the staff with performance indicators.

profit (n.) The corporate reason for being, but surprisingly tricky to define. An innocent young employee once asked a financial director if the company they both worked for was making a profit. "Hmm," said the director, pensively looking into the distance, "it depends on whom are you talking to…" There are peaks and troughs of cash flow, and a wily accountant can slide them around to amplify or flatten the overall picture. Different—and horribly complex—accounting standards operate on either side of the Atlantic. It can suit an international company not to make money in particular places and do spectacularly well in others. Local tax regimes are a consideration, but the decisive factor tends to be the figures on which the executive team will be assessed for their bonuses.

Such moving around of the margin is not difficult to contrive if different branches of an international organization trade with each other. If the same product is sold all over the planet, but made in just one place, the corporation can decide whether to ship it to its company in a particular territory at the cost of manufacture plus freight, or at a cost that represents a profit for the manufacturing division. See also **provisions**.

provisions (n.) Not consumables, but prudence in accounting. Suppose you have sold a million cake makers to the retail trade at a price that gives you a profit of a dollar per unit. Have you made a million bucks? No. Some of those cake makers will be sold to shops that go bust and cannot pay you. Some cake makers will be returned as faulty. What's more, to sell the million, you actually manufactured one and a half million, so you have half a million left in stock. Do you assume they will sell on, or might they be superseded by your Mark Two cake maker with the special icing attachment?

The prudent accountant will make provisions for these and other contingencies. A company that is under-provisioned may be overstating its profits. New management teams tend to take a bleak view of provisions, as losses can be blamed on the previous regime and writing the value of stock down to zero makes any continuing sales very profitable. Creative fiddling with provisions is a source of much financial bullshit.

Public Relations/PR (np.) Satan was not so bad; he just suffered from bad press. Corporations are similar. It's often easier to fix the perception of the problem than the problem itself.

pushing the envelope (phrase) This was used by the aviation pioneers of the 1940s and '50s who were extending the limits of their technology with every flight. It entered management speak with *The Right Stuff*, Tom Wolfe's 1979 book (made into a film in 1983) about the U.S. experimental aviation program. If you are Chuck Yeager breaking the sound barrier, the expression sounds authentic. On the other hand, if you are a corporate executive whose idea of danger is padding your expenses, it sounds ridiculous. See also **raising the bar**.

raising the bar (phrase) There are innumerable corporate expressions borrowed from sports. "Stepping up to the plate," "playing off the back foot," "a level playing field"… Business is not sport; it certainly is not Olympian, and it has never been sporting. Cheating is the norm. God knows what compulsory drug testing would reveal.

rationalize (v.) Like streamline, this may mean making your internal processes more intelligent, but it's a term that strikes a chill to the hearts of workers, too many of whom have been rationalized away. It is remarkable how much more clear-sighted management can be about duplication or inefficiency in ranks lower than their own.

[the] reality is… (catchphrase) One of those expressions that seem to combine melancholy knowledge of the world with a courageous determination to see it as it is. But everybody stands somewhere. Don't accept anyone's version of reality without examination. See also **realistic** under Political Bullshit.

red tape (np. imbued with animus) There is a lot of tiresome regulation; it would be naïve to deny it. But much of it was introduced in response to exploitation or some bloody and fatal accident. "Red tape" is a reference to the ribbons once used by lawyers to tie their papers, and, as if the legal connotation is not enough by itself to trigger a reflex of loathing, the word is often preceded by "bureaucratic." Dig further when some captain of industry whines about it. Is the red tape in question some government directive about the design of the ten-dollar bill, or is it about establishing a pension fund or replacing that slowly pulverizing asbestos roof in the machine room?

re-engineer (v.) See **restructure**.

relationship management (np.) Many service companies now use this term. For instance, you are unlikely to know your bank manager because the big banks removed much of the autonomy from branch managers in the 1980s. Instead, if you have enough money to be worth the effort, you may be awarded a *relationship* manager, usually someone with an affable telephone manner, big hair, and a portfolio of thousands of "clients." He or she will store your personal as well as professional information in a database running software like MS Contacts. This will enable the relationship manager to meter out a few minutes of specific charm ("How is little Molly? Did Scott get into Johns Hopkins? And Fido, the Labrador?") before getting around to your overdraft or selling you the latest product. A managed relationship is, by definition, false.

restructure (v.) Also **re-engineer**. If you are moving manufacturing to China or changing your factory so that instead of assembly-line construction, a single team makes, say, an entire car, then these radical-sounding verbs are apt. In practice, they are often grand euphemisms for shrinkage. See also **shed labor**.

rightsizing (gerund) A more nauseating variant of **downsizing**.

share (v.) In corporate circles, "share" is rarely applied to division of the spoils. More usually, the word is found masquerading as good practice in the mouths of senior executives seeking to inform. If the news is good, less pious terms are in order ("I want to tell you about the great big wad of currency that is your bonus..."). However, if an executive says "I'd like to share something with you," the more caring tone should trigger your Bullshit detectors. Whatever it is won't make your day.

shareholder value (np.) This is invoked as the one goal above all others that the directors of a company must achieve. Indeed it's their fiduciary duty, and when things go wrong, they carry these words like a shield borne into battle. If the directors have share options, their interests and those of the shareholders coincide. Is shareholder value the only measure of worth? What about the staff, the customers, the safety of the product? These are naïve questions.

shed labor (v.) Fire lots of people. The expression has the virtue of sounding honestly heartless.

short-termism (n.) This isn't a bullshitty term so much as a phenomenon. America's banks and venture capitalists are driven by it. After all, greed is good. If bankers lend money, they will want to get it back within two years, perhaps three if they are feeling visionary. The same applies more acutely to investors in equity. Almost always, their first question is this: What's the exit strategy? And the second is: When?

Corporations are even worse. Next Thursday is a far horizon. Everybody wants instant profits. One year's success becomes a rack on which the following year's figures will be tortured for—no matter how exceptional the circumstances—you cannot go backwards. This pressure tends to make CEOs reluctant to spend time building a business, especially if they fear that it will reduce the "bottom line" to the detriment of their year-end bonuses. (When it comes to personal bonuses, the bosses of corporations find embarrassment an entirely alien concept.) The fear of "not making your numbers" stalks the corridors of the head office like the Serial Killer in Residence. All kinds of short-term expedients are embraced in order to avoid becoming his next victim. Many a fine company (and not just in the U.S.) has been hollowed out by the relentless year-on-year pressure to improve the numbers. (See also **GAAS**.)

It is a tribute to the vitality and inventiveness of America that it is not more deeply in the custard. German and Japanese banks, in contrast, are prepared to lend for ten years, sometimes longer.

sign up to (v.) Endorse, acquiesce in, or agree to a decision. If a boss makes a mistake, he or she will say that "we all signed up to it." Committee decisions have been shown to be less reliable than individual ones, for the individuals who comprise the committee submerge their sense of responsibility in the collective. All kinds of group dynamics and politics take over in committees. A committee may take a decision about which, in the privacy of his or her mind, every member has doubts. See also **buy in**.

silo mentality (n.) Defensive thinking. But what's in the silo? Is it an ICBM or is the image more agricultural—in which case it could really be bullshit?

situation (n.) See **Political Bullshit**.

speak to (v.) In the boardrooms of the world, this unpretentious verb does not always mean that one human being talks to another. No, you speak to an issue. Or you may address an issue. Merely speaking *about* an issue would not have the same power. Of course, you do not say, "Good morning, issue" without a reckless disregard for your continuing employment. Why has this odd usage come in? It was originally heard in British courts from barristers describing the relevance of evidence, so perhaps its subsequent adopters yearned for the (putative) professionalism and precision of the law.

stochastic (adj.) In science, this describes a process that is random but has a calculable probability; hence, it can be repeated. Anybody using this term (other than a scientist or mathematician) is a black-belt Bullshitter.

strategic partnership (n./jargon) A dodgy co-venture in which both parties try to screw the other.

sub-optimal (adj.) Pretty crap, really.

SWOT (acronym) Strengths, Weaknesses, Opportunities, Threats. "We've got the funding, we've hockey-sticked the forecast, we've done a SWOT analysis, and it's looking good..." It makes sense to worry about every aspect of a business, especially a start-up, but we should beware of anybody deploying these acronyms without even the ghost of a grin. Business-school jargon is no substitute for brains.

synergy (n.) In corporations, the whole is not greater than the parts. Corporations have often grown by relentless acquisition. Eventually this leads to a disparate structure in which the cartel's octopoid fingers are in many different pies. But this is not a problem. No indeed, "synergy" will "add value" (see **value-added**). There is a technique for staying awake in corporate meetings by counting the incidence of coproemes. If you hear "synergy" five times in as many minutes, stand up with a cry of "Bullshit!"

town hall meetings (n.) Large gatherings where the boss tells the other ranks a bit about what is going on. Though there is a question and answer session afterwards (for there is a nod in the direction of freedom of speech), only someone with another job offer would risk causing embarrassment. Often there is a plant in the audience who has been primed to put a question for which a reply has been well rehearsed.

You might wonder what brings on this rush of frankness, so alien to the habits of a lifetime. Many town hall meetings result from takeover speculation. The boss and other equity holders stand to make millions (even billions), but the mechanics of acquisition are slow. It is vital for the share price (and hence those potential personal profits) that the business continues as a going concern while the purchaser's accountants are sifting through the books, throwing open the cupboard doors, and generally sniffing the assets (a process called due diligence). Hence the need to reassure the employees; it would be inconvenient if they bailed out early and damaged the company. After acquisition, the new owner can fire them, but that's not a problem for the current management.

transformational (adj.) Usually applied to leadership. Just hope that the charismatic bully at the top does not transform the organization into a melancholy memory.

transition (n. used as v.) Change job, but with added purpose...

valid (adj.) Once a philosophical term indicating that a formula was derived according to the rules, this is now a nuanced way of saying yes while leaving an escape route. "Hmm, I went along with this because I thought it was valid" suggests that I was persuaded by my colleague's orderly marshalling of the argument. I didn't actually *agree* as such, and now that I learn that some of the reasoning was slipshod or the premises faulty, I can renege with good conscience.

value-added (adj.) Theoretically, every link in the chain of manufacture and supply adds value (i.e., allows you to charge more), but the expression has become jargon for almost anything of which the management approves. There's even "value-added behavior"—good deeds without that uneasy hint of moral judgment.

viable (adj.) Sharing some of the same functions as **valid**, this word sounds as if the proposition in question had been subjected to deep analysis. It disguises the fact that many decisions are based on intuition or experience. These are both fallible, but probably less so than those purporting to be founded on cost-benefit analysis and similar techniques.

virtual (adj.) One of the many imports from information technology in which it has a specific meaning. A virtual environment, for instance, is a computer model of a world created by software engineers and graphic designers. In business circles, it has become a "hurrah word" (See Political Bullshit, p. **30**) unassailable by anybody older than thirty. A virtual organization is possible only in the age of email and the mobile phone. It is one without any—or the barest minimum of—permanent staff. A few highly skilled people from time to time recruit others from a network of contacts, thus avoiding the fixed costs of offices, rent, receptionists, bookkeepers, IT managers, and all the rest of humankind that used to be thought necessary.

Imagine you run an American company selling thingies in Europe. You manufacture them under license in China, import them with a shipper, distribute them under a contract with a logistics company, and market them using an agency. If anything goes wrong with your thingies, you have an arrangement with a call center in Delhi. Having no permanent structure, you are quick to respond to market changes. Any of the components can be dropped quickly, for your business is little more than a collection of contractual relationships. You aspire to be financially large and organizationally small—and thereby disgustingly profitable.

Pundits reckon virtual organizations may be the pattern of the future. The key people may find them exhilarating, but the third parties waiting to be paid will probably be less thrilled. The word carries a frisson of the edgy future. But what guarantees are there from a company that is a legal entity without physical assets?

vision (n.) Nobody wants a mere plan. It's not grand or messianic enough. Make sure you have a vision. Don't be like President Bush (Senior) who always had trouble with "the vision thing." If you simply cannot bring yourself to call your plan a "vision," at least call it a "strategy."

watering-hole meetings (n.) Hey, let's not be bound by the formality of meetings with their stultifying agendas, crippling politics, and minute-taking. Let's just gather around the coffee machine and creatively shoot the breeze. The hierarchies are suspended and your ideas will not be stolen. Honest.

we'll get back to you [though without specifying when] (cliché) In about half a century if you're lucky… Those unlucky in love report that "I'll call you" can have a similar function after one-night stands.

win-win situation (n./jargon) This expression comes from games theory, but it has been adopted by business in several senses. The formal meaning describes a decision in which the outcome is favorable whatever strategy is adopted. Yes, we've got the contract or no, we haven't, but participating in the game sends a signal perking up our share price... The term is also used for an actual deal advantageous to both participants. (This change in working practices makes life easier for the workers and brings savings to the company...) However, genuine "win-win situations" are rarer than a mandrake. The party who benefits most is invariably the one to deploy the jargon.

work hard, play hard (macho cliché) Heard on the lips of executives who reckon they have *droit de seigneur* over the sexier junior staff. Oddly, most of them don't work hard.

PART TWO

Political Bullshit:
I'm Glad You Asked Me That...

A man may take to drink because he feels himself a failure and then fail all the more completely because he drinks. It is rather the same thing that is happening to the English language. It becomes ugly and inaccurate because our thoughts are foolish, but the slovenliness of our language makes it easier for us to have foolish thoughts.

—George Orwell, essay in *Politics and the English Language* (1946)

Political language is fascinating. Its rhetorical devices are as old as oratory itself. The threefold repetition, for instance—"I will not trim, I cannot compromise, I shall not turn away"—has been rolling around the mouths of men in suits, or togas, since written records began. The double construction is also memorable: "not only convinced, but passionately convinced...", "tough on crime, tough on the causes of crime..." These tropes and tricks have a long history. Plato held that rhetoric (then a formal discipline) was ignoble. He saw it as an art of persuasion that is both manipulative and dishonest.

It is possible that consciousness and language evolved simultaneously. The British novelist and science fiction writer Brian Aldiss once observed that we are all living in the novel of our own lives. Without language enabling us to step outside the immediate and see ourselves in a wider context, would we be self-aware at all? Some philosophers, like Daniel Dennett, think that we would not be. Consciousness has recently become a very hot topic. Libraries of new books by mega-brains from many disciplines worry away at these complexities from different angles. As all the writers are condemned to use language itself to think about the role of language, they are straining at the intellectual equivalent of pulling themselves up by their bootstraps.

Skill with language goes to the heart of what it means to be human: it is our unique cognitive talent. The unusually fluent have enjoyed power over the rest of us for millennia. Mass communication allows those with the gift of the gab to exercise their influence with an unprecedented reach and speed. At the same time, these new media demand new abilities. Today great orators of the past, like Cicero or Churchill, would be simply too long-winded for a public attention span debauched by slick television and the staggering speed and density of advertisements. (And how would their speeches be rendered now? "We will fight in a multiplicity of environments including, but not limited to, France, beaches, landing grounds, fields…") Even Lincoln's Gettysburg address—though commendably brief—would be too much.

Now the sound bite rules. It's an art at which politicians train as joylessly as Olympic athletes. Avoid that stripy tie, it strobes. Look sincerely to camera, pause (so the editor has a cue for the cut), deliver some resonant snippet of bullshit, pause again (for the next cut). Your neatly packaged thirty seconds is much more likely than any complex message to make it to the TV news.

In democracies, the relationship between politicians and the media is rococo. Both parties loathe and need each other in equal measure. In an arena dominated by television, a politician who does not look good is unlikely to get elected. ("Mediagenic" is the decadent adjective on the lips of PR advisers.) The lesson of Nixon's five o'clock shadow in his first television debate with Kennedy was learned early and well.

Fortunately, in the English-speaking world, the media are—with a few dishonorable exceptions—not docile. Occasionally, some journalist will be complicit in presenting a story the way a politician wants it, but this will rarely be a matter of envelopes bulging with the green stuff. More likely it's a transaction in which sympathetic treatment is traded for exclusivity, access, or some future favor. Life is more complicated if the politicians own the media (Berlusconi in Italy) or have curried favor with some powerful proprietor by passing legislation helpful to his business interests (think of Rupert Murdoch).

But, the bias of their employers notwithstanding, many journalists maintain an admirable record of grilling sneaky and evasive politicians. In response, the suits have developed a repertoire of verbal conjuring tricks for sounding significant while saying nothing. When, in an interview, one of our leaders declares, "The important thing is…," it may or may not be important, but it will be the point that he or she wishes to make regardless of the question. It is not surprising how articulate politicians become after deploying this phrase, or its equivalent, for what follows is the message they have rehearsed.

Another trick at which politicians excel is the "hurrah word." Such words represent concepts so sacred that their mere presence in an utterance is intended to put it beyond criticism. Choice, freedom, liberty, life, God, family, democracy and/or democratic, human rights, equality—these are all first-division hurrah words often invoked to lend grandeur to some tawdry enterprise. A sentence like "Choice is a democratic freedom" strings together such a concatenation of hurrah words that—despite being absurdly vague—it sounds aphoristic and impregnable.

Hurrah words can be so burdened with assumptions and values that using them in argument can only produce vexation. Those on either side of the debate about abortion, for instance, call themselves "pro-life" and "pro-choice." It is not surprising that they are bitterly irreconcilable, for their language, the means by which they might achieve a meeting of minds, carries a built-in worldview. Second-division hurrah words include such goodies as innovative, multicultural, values (always deeply held), faith, and passion.

Teasing out the suppressed premises behind these expressions is not mere pedantry. When you attach a label to people, you are committing a political act whereby you legitimize your behavior towards them. At its most extreme, this can be psychopathic. Pol Pot, in the grip of an insane version of communism, believed that whole categories of human beings were bourgeois, and hence parasitic. He murdered millions in an attempt to make a society more closely resembling the simplicities of dogma. William S. Burroughs, the gray-skinned junkie author of *Naked Lunch*, observed that language is the ultimate control system legislating thought, feeling, and what he rather disturbingly called *apparent* sensory perception.

George Orwell skewered it in 1946. Sloppy language is the ally of insincerity. If the vocabulary is debased, eventually there will be distinctions we can no longer make, subtleties we can no longer think. We forfeit the right to protest if we devalue the currency of political discourse.

---

accountability (abstract n.) A mysterious virtue that all politicians claim to possess until the time comes to demonstrate it.

activist (n.) Is anybody who can be bothered to turn up an activist? Is it helpful to describe a parent who attends a meeting at her child's school as an activist? Politicians and journalists reach for the same word when describing a zealous Trot scheming for a new world order. The word is preceded by the adjective **militant** often enough for the association to linger like departed cheese. That residual activist-equals-radical equation makes protests attributed to activists easier to ignore than those undertaken by citizens. "Participant" seems too bland. It's a pity there isn't some less tendentious term for somebody, say, attending a meeting about a local issue.

adjustment center (n./prison jargon) Solitary confinement.

adverbs (grammatical term) Adverbs can be makeweights adding emphasis, phony judiciousness, or the appearance of conviction. "We are *somewhat* concerned...I am *totally* committed...The party is *utterly* opposed..." We all do it in direct speech to lend color and emphasis, and to give ourselves time to think. Politicians, on the other hand, have speechwriters whose use of such techniques is deliberate.

One adverb that is pale with exhaustion is "ironically." Radio and TV reporters use it frequently as a synonym for "in contrast," "with unfortunate aptness," or sometimes just "next." Most of the time, "ironically" serves as an all-purpose link suggesting the sardonic crispness of the reporter's analysis.

agenda (n. pl.) Something interesting has happened to this once innocent word. Pedants may fret that "agenda," like "data," "media," and, more painfully, "phenomena," is one of those plurals that is often treated as singular. Strictly speaking, you cannot have "an agenda" (an *agendum*, maybe).

The dictionary definition focuses on the idea of a list of items or ideas for consideration. Perhaps the lexicographers at the *OED* will have clocked the first time someone described a politician as having a "hidden agenda"—intentions, probably creepy, other than those openly declared. This telling image stuck in the public's imagination. By some curious process of semantic compression, in the right context we can hear "hidden" even when the qualifier is not uttered. A politician with his own agenda is untrustworthy whereas one with a **vision** (see Corporate Bullshit) is admirable. However, the word is now so overused that even this sinister subtext is fading. In the 2004 television debate between President Bush and Senator Kerry (though both were so grimly over-rehearsed that "debate" seems hardly the right word), the candidates used the word as a synonym for "plan." Perhaps the idea they hoped to convey was that they execute their intentions as efficiently as ticking items off a list.

Meetings without an agenda can be a torment. However, there is a bullshit trick for suggesting that such encounters are not inchoate but instead open to creative possibilities. Just describe them as "unstructured."

ask [whomever] that (coded phrase) Politicians attack their rivals with the finesse of a hand grenade, but they are usually inhibited from calling each other liars except at election time. It's not parliamentary language, and besides, it could set a disastrous precedent. So, if questioned by a sharp interviewer about something tricky or some clearly mendacious behavior committed by another, the code is to say, "You must ask him that. It's not for me to say."

average (n. and adj.) An average is a mathematical notion, never spotted in real life. We should chortle when we hear someone claiming to speak on behalf of this creature; it's like saying you represent the unicorn lobby. (See also **average, mean, and median** under Crapmatics.)

Beltway bandit (n.) A term for a Washington insider who leaves the government (the Beltway is the highway that loops around Washington) and—for much, much more money—immediately starts working for an industry or a lobby group about which his or her previous incarnation provided specialist knowledge and contacts.

benchmarking (n.) A fashionable word for comparative research (see **more research needs to be done**). The idea is pinched from engineering. A horizontal lathe will have a steel scale marked on to the bench so that the operator can machine to a precise measure. Some politicians now "benchmark" in the sense that during parliamentary holidays, they travel overseas on well-funded freebies to see what standards other countries set when dealing with a particular problem. You have to be willing, of course, to think **outside the box** (see Corporate Bullshit). Acapulco or Tuscany may well have lessons to teach us about single mothers in California or library funding in Louisiana.

best value (government jargon) A neat conjunction of hurrah words meaning the cheapest. Thus, our children eat best-value school meals that cost fifty cents and consist mainly of the likes of Turkey Twizzlers that look like greasy, helical bowel movements extruded from the nozzle of a machine. As a result of privatization (see **PFI**), many schools are locked into long-term contracts requiring them to feed these to generations of school kids.

bilateral (adj.) Many talks and negotiations are between two parties. If the U.S. State Department is haggling with Italy over whether "Parma" in Parma ham is a toponym or a generic, the talks are obviously bilateral. The word injects gravitas.

bourgeois (adj. and n.) In feudal France, this had a precise definition to do with solvency and length of residence, but in recent times, it has become impossible to separate this now unfashionable word from its historical baggage. It means much more than middle class—however that is defined—for it implies that this category of person may be stodgy, overly preoccupied with the opinions of neighbors, comfortably off and determined to stay that way, conventional but possibly just a little warped underneath…

In Marxist theory, the bourgeoisie, despised by the aristocracy, was the great exploiter of the **proletariat**. A complex of social and sexual attitudes is implied by the term, with the result that its use may say more about the speaker than the people to whom he is attaching the label. A politician using the term might have warmed it up in a compost heap of half-hidden ideology. The words "petit bourgeois" are more obviously steeped in theory and thus more of a giveaway.

capability gap (np.) We can't do it. See **credibility gap**.

charm offensive (np.) This started life as a witty oxymoron, but familiarity has inured us to its absurdity.

choice (n.) One of the most potent hurrah words in the politician's armory, almost as powerful as **freedom**, with which it is often joined. Its primary meaning is the ability to make an unforced decision from a range of options. By some kind of leakage, the word enjoys the connotations of a secondary meaning—select, exclusive, desirable ("a choice morsel"). Choice is self-evidently a Good Thing with a history of political philosophy behind it that goes back to Adam Smith and, more recently, Hayek, Friedman, Reagan, and Thatcher. Choice is holy because free markets need it to function, and markets (as some believe) are the mechanism that regulates all.

But choice has to be informed to be rational, and the options from which a choice is made have to be practical. The choice between a trip to the supermarket and a trip to Hawaii is silly. We are good at choosing a pair of jeans. Many brands are offered, and plenty of limiting factors (size, budget, fit) come into play before those clever marketing people have a chance to get at our unconscious needs. If it matters to you that your backside carries a fashionable label, you can be satisfied without eye-watering expense or having to master too much esoteric knowledge. You can make an informed choice.

However, the same does not apply to services such as education. In any area, there's unlikely to be more than a couple of local state schools; information about them may not be readily available and what there is will need interpretation. Private schooling costs a fortune. Also, schools are not mobile; they are fixed on one site—and usually so are you. Rather than exercise choice by bussing your children for hours every day, wouldn't you prefer to be guaranteed excellence by the school around the corner? The range of choice may also be a bit chimerical. With schools, for instance, the quality and convenience are likely to lie on a pretty steep gradient. You might not want your fourth and fifth choices at all, despite the fact that some daft form has forced you to identify them.

Even Adam Smith recognized what he called "the duties of Princes" to provide what the market cannot. Leaving aside the question of the profligate waste of resources in competitive economies, if you are buying an electric kettle, it makes sense that there are ten manufacturers vying for your dollar. When you plug it in, however, you do not have ten plugs bearing the logos of different energy suppliers. This argument applies even more tellingly to healthcare. With any luck, your need for the local hospital will be intermittent enough to render research into its virtues neurotic. If, having stepped carelessly into the path of a truck, you are comatose in a pool of your own ketchup, you are not equipped to make a choice. The "invisible hand" of the market just does not work in all contexts. Some services are natural monopolies to be run for the public good.

All this raises the question of political priorities. See also **freedom**.

clarification (n.) Somebody has been caught telling a lie the size of Mount Rushmore. Obviously, it cannot be called a lie; "misstatement" slips down the public's throat more comfortably. But whatever it is called, it cannot be retracted without confessing to an acute attack of mendacity. Such a course is unthinkable, so instead we are treated to the sight of some unfortunate press officer or spokesperson, shiny with sweat under the studio lights, issuing a "clarification."

clerical error (np.) For goodness sake, the subtext goes, you cannot hold *me* responsible for the mistake made by some nitwit so junior that I have scarcely heard of his grade, yet alone the individual. Once upon a time, politicians did not blame their civil servants. Now they dump on them profusely. If the screw-up reflects policy, then "clerical error" is a lie.

The government's clerical errors, once set in concrete, are hell to change. Unless they are corrected in every file, the system perversely resets the original mistake.

commission fees (n.) In large export deals, a euphemism for bribes. See also **old-fashioned conversation**.

communication problem (np.) See **presentation**.

community (n.) This word (from the Old French) has many meanings. In medieval times, it signified the commons—the ordinary folk without noble rank. Then the meaning shifted to embrace people from particular districts. Before the rise of public and personal transport, everybody in a small area would willy-nilly know everyone else. Villages would also have local rights to land held in common which they needed to defend against the depredations of the powerful; thus there emerged the idea of a community of interest. This important meaning is based more on a shared need than on geography. Now the meanings have converged. The word has acquired an aura of warmth suggesting a dense social fabric in which the people not only know each other, but look out for one another's interests. Similarly, there's a sentimental glow attached to the word "neighborhood."

Politicians often invoke the community and claim to be "in touch" with it. In modern cities, the pattern of acquaintanceship is dispersed and not based on the accident of proximity. Indeed, for some urbanites, the anonymity of the neighbors is a virtue. Cities contain many "communities" that interact like those shoals of fish that can swim through each other without a single individual touching another from a different species. What is a community when you do not know, or care to know, who lives in the house next door? And what of other communities—of merchant bankers, homosexuals, car drivers…? Are their needs and appetites really so similar that "community," a comforting wooly blanket, covers them all? That said, there is no obvious substitute for this hard-working word.

concerns (n.) Not bullshit exactly, but insipid and all-purpose. You can have concerns about anything from nuclear proliferation to biodegradable paper bags. A politician may express concern to show he or she cares, but he or she doesn't have to do anything.

In the social services, "concerns" demonstrate anxiety of a non-specific nature. Social workers are trained to list those "on concern" to cover themselves in case of subsequent disaster. For the insider, "serious concerns" are alarming code words. A family about whom the social worker has serious concerns might well appear on the TV news in a horror show of blood and incest.

consensus (n.) Politicians often claim a consensus for any opinion they hold dear. How do they know? If they've conducted a poll with a large, demographically weighted sample and rigorous statistical analysis, they may be entitled to use the word. (Such polls are extremely difficult in practice. See Crapmatics.) Otherwise, it's just an expression of their own opinion. (See also **majority**.) "Consensus politics" has distinct meanings depending on whether or not you approve. Sometimes it represents an admirable attempt to find the widest possible agreement over some question. The term can also be heard with contempt—as just an insipid occupation of the middle ground, devoid of principle or conviction.

consultancies (n.) A device whereby politicians represent special interests—in other words, they are bribes of a respectable nature.

consultation (n.) Consultations are invariably full and wide-ranging. They come in two flavors. The first and more common is window-dressing that helps to validate a decision long since taken (building new airport runways falls into this category). The second is when the politician hasn't a clue what to do and hopes the consultation will tell him or her what the public will dislike the least.

consumer (n.) We are all consumers now—of goods, services, and resources. As such, our interests are protected by **rights**, commercial guarantees, associations, fiercely ferreting journalists, TV programs, and many volumes of law. "Consumer" and "consumerism" are gravid with inadvertent honesty. In other contexts, consumption implies destruction and waste (consumed by fire, by tuberculosis…). As a species, we're consuming the planet at a suicidal rate. But in a political or economic setting, the word enjoys more positive connotations: the little man, defended by consumer legislation from menacing cartels, can now expect his daily bread to be unadulterated and his electric toaster to be safe. It is this benign aura and a certain sense of no-nonsense commerce that a politician steals when he uses the word: despite my many directorships, consultancy fees, and lobby lunches (says the subtext), I'm on your side, keeping an eye on those giant combines that might be sneaking shoddy goods or iffy services on to the market.

But the word is all-purpose. You can consume a financial product as grammatically as you can a cream cake. The word carries just a hint of patronizing contempt (rather like "punter") when enunciated by a politician in a beautiful suit. You're a consumer, but I am a buyer, investor, traveler, customer, client, contractor of services…or generally a more precisely defined creature.

context (n.) See **out of context**.

credibility gap (np.) We know they're lying or are simply unable to do what they said they could do. Something inhibits us from saying so directly—probably the fact that as professional Bullshitters, the politicians deceive themselves before they lie to us.

crisis (n.) A word routinely abused. All kinds of spats between celebrities are now crises. We crave drama, and the tabloid press has to provide it, especially on a slow news day. The cream-bun cholesterol crisis? The Beverly Hills hairstylists' crisis? Etymologically, the word implies a decisive moment. Strictly speaking, problems with a historical dimension (e.g., the pensions crisis) are not crises. Perhaps such pedantry can only be expressed in the strangulated voice of a serious nerd. Repetition has desensitized us to this smashing word.

culture (n.) A major hurrah word; the 600-pound gorilla of the lexical world. It's anything any large group of people has done for long enough. What does it mean? Everything. Massively useful in defense, the word induces panic and paralysis in social workers all over the world. See **multicultural**.

dangling participle (grammatical form) It is strange how certain constructions carry a subliminal message. What is it about a dangling participle that makes it so sonorous and somehow *sincere*? It seems the more truncated a slogan, the pithier it appears and the less it specifies, for without syntax, there is no shape to the idea.

decisions [difficult] (np.) The subtext goes like this: I've had the guts to make a decision, even though it could not please everyone. If the decision is seen later as immoral, illegal, or an appalling cock-up, at least I've had the courage to bear the burden of difficult decision-making. Thus I turn error into heroism.

democracy (n.) This concept is not monolithic. There are many different versions. Is it a direct democracy—probably only possible on a small scale—or a representative one? The great eighteenth-century parliamentarian and writer Edmund Burke had much to say about whether MPs were representatives or delegates. Does a democracy have an electoral college system so that—as in 2000—the President of the United States could be elected without enjoying a majority of the popular vote? Is there universal franchise—and how democratic is it if large fractions of the enfranchised (nearly half in the case of the 2000 election) cannot be bothered to record a preference?

Communist states often call themselves people's democracies, a description of unbearable irony but one which is meant to distinguish a one-party system that everybody can join from capitalist democracies with all the advantages they confer on the rich. Where does democratic protection reside from day to day? In a constitution? Not all democracies have one. Or is it that the judiciary is independent of the state, the secret police under control, and the media diverse, energetic, and relatively unconstrained save by the interests of the proprietors and the laws of defamation?

In practice, "democratic rights" such as freedom of speech are already limited by legally enforceable rules about libel or incitement to racial hatred. We live in societies that outlaw many types of activity from murder to driving too quickly—and we should be grateful, for we would not relish inhabiting a world in which we left it to people's innate sweet nature to make them behave well. So when it is asserted sententiously that something is alien to our democracy, or is profoundly undemocratic, our response should not be a reflex based upon the sacramental nature of the word. Instead we must ask that dreary question: what *exactly* is the aspect of our complicated social organization to which reference is being made?

deregulation (n.) A minor hurrah word. Let's strip away all those idiotic rules and restrictions, it seems to say, and free up those enterprises to do what they do best. Despite many counter-examples, an enduring superstition holds that private companies are efficient because they operate in the jungle of capitalist rapacity: if they were not, they would soon be eaten. Even if that were always true, how is efficiency defined in the context of public infrastructure? For instance, it might not be cost-efficient to run rural bus routes, but it might be desirable. State-owned businesses, on the other hand, are supposed to be inhabited exclusively by happy, unquestioning paper-shufflers, all smugly insulated from the icy blasts of the market.

Neither of these attitudes carries much conviction. The most notorious deregulation in recent political history was that of the airline industry under President Reagan. The ferocity of the competition that followed was extraordinary, and many fewer airlines were left serving the public when it was over.

If you are less than sure about the virtues of private interests running essential public services, you might describe such businesses using a value-laden word like "unlicensed." It's interesting to contrast the hurrah word "deregulated" with the negative connotations of "unregulated."

diversity (n.) Used to refer to a mix of races. The word is also found a lot in educational circles. Why do the users feel the need for code? See also **race**.

dogma (n.) The other guy has dogma, but you have passion.

élite/élitism (n.) These words are now so thoroughly incorporated into English that they are often written without that French acute accent, and just as frequently pronounced "ee-leet" rather than "ay-leet." Meaning a choice or select group, élite always suggested a sense of exclusivity, despite the fact that in English the term is often just applied to the best at any given activity. An élite bunch of mathematicians suggests nothing about snotty attitudes; it says only that they are brilliant at math.

Politicians—especially on the left—tend to use the term in a derogatory social sense to exploit the politics of jealousy. For them, the word does not indicate excellence, but is calculated to license those of us who are not members of an élite to loathe the false superiority of those who are. Minority cultural tastes, especially if expensive (opera, for example), are often described as elitist, as if thereby indubitably a Bad Thing—though some have argued the opposite on the same grounds. Given that the infamous bell curve can map most human abilities, there will always be élites, and the aim of an equitable social system should be to give everybody an equal chance of joining one.

embedding (n.) In the last Gulf War, journalists were "embedded" in units of the army. The word is comforting. Those favorable associations of the root word, *bed*, work away behind the scenes. Protection, warmth, duvets, pleasure... Quite apart from any restrictions imposed by the military censor, would an "embedded" reporter, as part of the military team, feel entirely free to comment? Is he or she as much a third-party observer as an old-fashioned war correspondent on the front line? Would Hemingway have been "embedded"? See also **rendition**.

empowerment (n.) George W. Bush's presidency has seen more centralized, unreviewable power under the control of the executive branch than any other recent administration, and yet it talks constantly of empowerment. It seems to mean letting people get on with what they've always done. Given the mania for interference and targets, this is altogether dishonest.

equality (abstract n. and powerful hurrah word) "We hold these truths to be sacred and undeniable: that all men are created equal..." said Thomas Jefferson, a slave owner. Men are not created equal.

We humans come in many varieties: large, small, brainy, dumb, healthy, weedy, and so on. The complex shuffling of the genetic pack produces geniuses and nitwits, sometimes in the same family, as in the case of Beethoven, who was preceded by many idiotic siblings. There's no point in grieving about it in jealous frenzy. (Sometimes, damn it, nature's hand seems to slip and you come across people both brilliant and beautiful. Is that fair?) If you encounter people cleverer than you are, good luck to them—it's a lottery. Perhaps one day we will all be able to modify ourselves using GM technology. Until that happens, we are not equal, but we can do our utmost to ensure that irrelevancies, such as the light absorption qualities of the epidermis, the shape of our noses, the possession of breasts, and so on, do not deny us access to the best of what society has to offer.

errors of judgment (often a euphemism) Politicians will sometimes admit to errors of judgment. Nobody's perfect, after all, and wouldn't we be unreasonable if we expected our leaders to be so? There's an air of harmless abstraction about the phrase, as if one were wrangling over the merits of Raphael's use of color. Tactically, politicians will put their hands up to confess to a lesser charge of an error of judgment if the alternative—corruption, for example—is more damaging. See also **mistakes**.

expert (n.) Defined by the American educator Nicholas Butler as someone who knows more and more about less and less, an expert is always expensive and often wrong. No two will agree. In politics, if you're paralyzed by indecision or ignorance (not that the latter is often inhibiting), calling in experts sounds like you're doing something. It also has the benefit—rather like **consultation** and research (see **more research needs to be done**)—of postponing the decision.

fact (n.) Often found in phrases like "The fact of the matter is…" or "It is a fact that…" A fact is a proposition about the world that is the case. Sometimes politicians will say "the true facts"—presumably to distinguish them from some other sort? "Plain facts" are also popular. "Assertion" or "opinion" would be more to the point.

faith (n./hurrah word) Many politicians find it expedient to advertise their faith. It is usually profound, deeply felt, and/or learned from their decent old mom and pop.

But what is someone saying who in every interview trails his credentials as a Christian, Muslim, Zoroastrian, or Jew? Trust me, for I have religious values and must be a good person? Trust me, for I have the humility to believe in something greater? You do not have to believe in a god to be honest. The public should demand more convincing tests of probity than attendance at some place of worship.

Perhaps there's a more subtle message: trust me, because with faith comes certainty. Yet decisiveness is not a religious trait, and besides, doubt may be richer and more useful in a complex world. Certainty buttressed by religious conviction evolves into zeal and incites many horrors. Surely the suppressed premise is not: trust me, because the omnipotent entity that created the whole universe intended me to occupy this job?

The more likely explanation for the public affirmation of faith is that the politician has identified a demographically powerful group whose votes he needs. Sociologists (though bullshit-prone themselves) tell us that loose affiliations of people who define themselves in terms of religion will often (though not invariably) share a similar set of opinions over a wide range of issues. This clustering of attitudes is useful for a politician pressing a populist "hot button," for he or she can appear to be expressing a view held by many constituents.

family (n.) In U.S. rhetoric, families tend to be God-fearing and hardworking. In the UK, they are hardworking and decent. The warm image of the nuclear family has been kept alive by politicians, sitcom writers, and advertisers. Mom and Dad are married (for the only time and to each other). They are prosperous, middle-aged, and still sexy. They love each other, though they might occasionally crack fond jokes about each other's eccentricities. Their two happy, well-adjusted, and clearly bright children adore them and are adored in turn. In large kitchens opening on to sunny gardens, the family eats together in a golden glow of cornflakes, affection, and witty banter. In the background, an invisible audience chortles with mechanized merriment.

Do we need the census figures to tell us that such families are a minority of households?

fast track (n. and v.) Trust us. We will torture our civil servants to drop the rest of their duties until the media spotlight has moved on to some other issue. Of individual careers, fast-tracking could mean a plenitude of things. The President's former lover? The repayment of a political debt? Grooming an ally? The need for a token woman/African American/working-class person at the President's side? It's even possible that somebody of exceptional talent has been identified.

[My] fellow Americans...(Presidential State of the Union cliché) What is going on here? Not even de Gaulle at his most messianic started his speeches with "My fellow Frenchmen..." (it was "Men and women of France..."). "Fellow" suggests a **community**, even a **family**—an idea difficult to reconcile with that extraordinary American vitality that flows from its wholesale importation of different cultures. If the USA is a giant family, then the President aspires to be the father figure. "Our great nation" is an expression that also reliably appears in such speeches. The message is parental reassurance.

finesse (n. used as v.) "We'll finesse this one past the committee..." "Finesse" in this context is a way of saying that we will burden the issue with so much bullshit that the committee will not spot it for what it is.

focus group (np.) Our leaders assure us that they are in the grip of a vision; they will change the world and make it a better, fairer, and generally more cuddly place. They should be haranguing us passionately about what to do. Instead they invest time and brain power not on much-needed legislation but on taking soundings about how some idea will go down with the public. Never mind what ought to be done—will it play well and keep the politicians in power?

freedom (abstract n.) This is the politician's most powerful hurrah word. Yet, given that people are prepared to die for the idea, it is remarkably ill defined.

Psychoanalyst and social theorist Erich Fromm wrote a wonderful book called *The Fear of Freedom* in which he made an important distinction between "freedom from" and "freedom to." "Freedom to" puts us to the test. We become responsible for our lives—and that brings many anxieties. "Freedom from"—from fear, pain, hunger, and so on—is much more desirable. History shows how ambivalent people can feel when a tyranny that offered the majority "freedom from" (but at terrible cost to dissenters) is replaced by a system with more "freedom to" but little or no state provision. Unimaginably, you can find Russians nostalgic for the days of Stalin.

The existentialists bang on in similar fashion. We are free, they say, but everywhere we seek out conventions in order to trammel our lives. That way, we can trundle on in a trance of unreflective comfort without facing decisions that would force us to define ourselves. By avoiding freedom, we live in "bad faith." (*Mauvaise foi*—like so much philosophical bullshit, it sounds better in French.)

Those living under a dictatorship do not need Sartre to tell them what they have lost. Fortunately, many of us will never experience such conditions. We live in relatively free societies—but they are societies governed by law, and much of that is concerned with limiting freedom. As communal creatures living in huge aggregations, we cannot function with unlimited license. Are you free to play your Metallica collection on your 5,000-watt stereo in the small hours despite the anguish of the neighbors? But would it be reasonable to do so up to midnight? One individual's freedom has to be compatible with another's, and the question becomes where to draw the line. Vast quantities of case law relate to the exact geography of that line. It wavers between civil liberty and security, license and censorship, freedom of expression and defamation, free market economics and consumer protection. Individuals draw the line at different points. The contemporary British philosopher John Gray succinctly observes that freedom is a social artifact.

Unless the context is imprisonment or some grim totalitarian regime, the word "freedom" on the lips of a politician is often a bludgeon to stun us into not thinking precisely. See also **choice** and **deregulation**.

full and frank (diplomatic adj. phrase) The negotiators are bitterly irreconcilable; they loathe each other with unimaginable passion. After days of wrangling, they struggle to issue an anodyne statement as bland as a bread roll. "Full and frank" is one step away from screaming invective and throwing the Perrier at each other. See also **robust**.

-gate (factitious word) Every scandal is now a something-gate. The reference, of course, is to the Watergate scandal that brought down the presidency of Richard Nixon. Reaching for the suffix is a forlorn, or maybe just lazy, attempt to make something sound just as important. Iran-gate—maybe. But Nipple-gate? (Janet Jackson showed an elegant breast at a Superbowl half-time show.) Would Othello have suffered Droppedhankie-gate?

God (n.) A mysterious entity that some people believe created the universe. God also provides the authority for many of our behavioral rules and acts as a guarantor of post-mortem survival of the spirit. This potent hurrah word is often invoked to lend cosmic significance or moral certainty to some iffy enterprise. God is always on the side of the speaker. See also **faith**.

guidelines (n.) Conforming to guidelines is vaguely desirable, but not enforceable by law. They are widely ignored by everybody except those who think they might want to get back into the game and thus have to have an unblemished record. See also **Beltway bandit**.

heritage (n.) Eighteenth-century buildings appendaged to shops selling kitsch. Let us by all means cherish this stuff, but not at the cost of turning the country into a giant theme park.

More broadly, heritage stands for values invoked by those preying on our fear of change. The past was a Golden Age of craftsmanship, grand architecture, shared values, national pride, and lovably eccentric aristocrats. The proles were happy for they knew their place. Despite the squalor and disease, they enjoyed the richness and warmth of a close community. What's more, not so long ago they could leave their front doors open, knowing that nobody would steal from them. Nineteenth-century observers like William Cobbett and Henry Mayhew provide antidotes to such sentimental waffle. See also **tradition**.

high net worth (np./jargon) Individuals with high net worth are rich.

hypothetical (adj.) A useful term to describe the kind of searching question that will not under any circumstances be answered.

I am glad you asked me that... (catchphrase in interviews) Because it gives me an opportunity to come out with my rehearsed spiel regardless of the question. If the right question is not asked, the politician being interviewed will say "Yes, but the important thing to understand is..." and then segue back into his sub-routine.

I am not persuaded [of the wisdom of such a course...] (catchphrase) Obviously I've listened carefully to all the arguments—so unlike somebody who merely does not agree.

I hear what you're saying... [usually followed by "but..."] (catchphrase) But I think—though in an affably non-confrontational way—that it's crap.

inappropriate (adj.) Many politicians are lawyers who resort to this impressive word to avoid defamation or self-incrimination. To say Senator

Weisenheimer's behavior was "inappropriate" presents less legal risk than saying he is a corrupt toad so crooked he cannot lie straight in bed. "My actions were inappropriate" looks like a confession, but is far less damaging than almost any other pejorative adjective one can think of. Venal? Greedy? Unprincipled?

Refusing to answer a question on the grounds that it is inappropriate implies that some subtlety is at work, a breach of confidentiality perhaps, or that the media are once again probing a triviality when all the politician wants to do is get back to the serious issues.

initiative (n.) Initiatives are always "launched," just as cuts are invariably "severe." The dictionary definition suggests a new start. But what is an initiative? It is self-referential. You launch one by the act of stating that you are doing so.

inoperative (adj.) A word made infamous at the time of Watergate. An inoperative statement is a lie.

in some sense (adv. phrase) A clever makeweight. For an agile mind, in some sense anything is true.

insurgents (n.) An example of how labeling is a political act. Insurgents sound as if they deserve all they get. Maybe they do. The dictionary definition is those in revolt or rebellion against an established government. But what if there is not an established government? Perhaps a precise account of the many groups and belief systems covered by the term—assuming there is such knowledge—may be too complicated or more disturbing than the one-size-fits-all label. When casualty figures are published by the military, one suggestion for a synonym for insurgents is "passersby."

investment (n.) Spending, as in "We're investing in schools."

involve (v.) Usually as a past participle, this is lesser bullshit by virtue of being so all-purpose and non-specific. "Sorry, I'm late—I was involved in an accident..." Did you have an accident, witness one, hold some poor wretch's hand while he expired in a welter of blood, or just get snarled up in the resulting traffic jam?

Politicians who are involved in an issue actually know what it is. Deeply involved? They have also read an article in the *Washington Post*.

inward investment (jargon) This is straightforward when it refers to foreign interests opening offices or building factories in your country—though they might be doing so because they have already assassinated the domestic competition. However, it acquires a tinge of bullshit when used by the government itself. Even when inward investment looks innocent, you have to wonder what makes your country an attractive place. Could it be large grants and **flexible** (see Corporate Bullshit) labor laws?

irony (n.) See "ironically" in **adverbs** and also **post-modern irony** under Professional Bullshit.

-ism (suffix for abstract nouns) To the extent that it purports to be an organized system of thought, whereas the world is untidy and irredeemably complicated, any "ism" is Bullshit. Sometimes the suffix is added to suggest that something represents a general phenomenon. What is "managerialism," for example?

-ist (all-purpose suffix) This spread from reasonable if ill-defined terms like sexist, via ageist, to any composite word that the user wanted to suggest implied prejudice. "Youthist," "fatist," even "beardist" have all been spotted. This verbal tic has become so over-used that it can only be indulged as a self-conscious parody of political correctness, a target satirized to the point of fatigue.

it has been pointed out (phrase) Similar expressions include "some argue...," "there's evidence to suggest...," "many are of the opinion...," "arguably..." They all mean: I think, but I'm waiting to see how it goes down with the audience before committing myself.

joined-up government or **thinking** (np.) Joined-up government is supposed to allow different departments to work together with the ensemble precision of Charlie Parker and Dizzy Gillespie on a good day. It is an admirable aspiration. The trouble is that the organizations themselves are colossal and staffed by *Homo sapiens*, a territorial higher primate. What's more, the whole structure of government is based on ministries, powerful institutions headed by cabinet politicians jealous of their fiefdoms. Something far more radical than a liaison committee will be needed if we are ever to enjoy joined-up government.

Different departments not only fail to talk to each other but often seem to be pursuing incompatible aims. How else can we understand the government's encouragement of sustainable energy sources in order to meet its carbon emissions target under the Kyoto treaty, while at the same time it is bulldozing new runways and airport expansion schemes through the planning process?

judgmental (adj.) Judgmental has come to mean censorious, swift to condemn. Why? There's a relativism implicit in the word. Things cannot be said to be better or worse than other things—merely different—and those who are confident in their judgments are arrogant. The next time somebody condemns you for being judgmental, try responding: "Too right. So how do you get through life?" Of course we must strive not to be unkind or bigoted, but the fear of making judgments has left us adrift. Politicians find the word helpful in deflecting criticism from an opponent. Much used also in psychobabble.

Law of Inverse Seniority, the (political expedient) If something unpopular must be announced, the President regrets that he or she has an unbreakable schedule of engagements elsewhere and is unavailable for interview. Instead the government fields someone of whom the public has never heard. The more loathsome the message, the less senior the spokesperson. An announcement of thermonuclear war would probably be delegated to the cleaners.

league table (n.) We live in a society obsessed with ranking things. This week's top five supermodels without a cocaine habit, the top ten vodka martinis, the twenty most romantic weekend breaks for spoiled brats... The habit has spread into politics, where charts purport to provide the gritty information essential for making well-informed, market-based choices.

Schools and hospitals are ranked relentlessly. Numbers look like hard data, but they are not. (For more about this, see Crapmatics.) How does a hospital measure performance? The number of patients treated? Does a chap who comes into outpatients for dialysis twice a week for years count as one? Or do you count procedures? Or waiting lists? If so, what matters? The length of the list or the time people spend on it? The latter has led hospital managers—whose budgets may depend on achieving targets—to reduce waiting lists by doing the quickies first. Five hundred ingrown toenails may be fixed while ten hip replacements hang about...

And who keeps account? Nurses and doctors are frantic. Better employ someone. But this will trigger the accusation that the finite budget is being spent on hiring people with titles like (this is an actual example) "Quality and Audit Supervision Manager." These jobs are what the opposition calls "bureaucracy" and the government describes as making sure the taxpayer gets value for every penny.

But what if you suspect the figures are being massaged? Then you will need a professional from one of the big audit companies to check every figure (and the expenses in an auditor's brain clock up faster than a New York taxi meter). In the end, can you ever compare like with like? The geriatric oncology hospital may be doing invaluable work, but its mortality rate will inevitably be higher than the infirmary down the road that stitches up battered boozers on Friday nights.

By definition, numbers are a notation with a built-in order. Imagine three 1,000-digit numbers, identical except for the very last figure. The difference between them would be many orders of magnitude less than the ratio between one atom and the observable universe, but we could still rank them. Psychologically, wouldn't we be inclined to favor the number which came out at the top of the chart? Numbers allow us to do that, but that does not mean they reflect any meaningful distinction in the world.

This preoccupation with measurement—presented as a public service—is predicated on anxiety and suspicion. The President, dropped into a huge job after an election, cannot master so much detail in time to feel confident enough about the brief. His permanent subordinates know much more than the President, who fears he may be conned, for his own seedy values are those he imputes to others. In response, the politician will damn well force people to quantify performance. The effect on morale and the public purse is incalculable. See also **delivery**.

Yet obviously schools and hospitals do differ in quality. There are no short cuts. If we do not know someone strategically placed to make a shrewd judgment on our behalf, we have to be prepared to dig deeply into the charts and invest time in analysis. See also **targets**.

liberal (n. and adj.) Summons images of the dated stereotype of a liberal, a sandal-wearing beardy with an important bottom and a sensible pullover. He is a pleasant enough creature, able to breed in captivity, though herbivorous and gently ineffectual. He simply does not understand that human beings are driven by self-interest. The liberal maintains that it *is* self-interested to want to live in a society that is not so inequitable that it needs a vast apparatus of social enforcement to contain its contradictions. This argument is dismissed as soppy.

In fact western liberalism has given us the abolition of slavery, an improvement in the position of women in society, the end of child labor, rights for workers, and much else besides. The positive aspects of the word—tolerance, openness to change, generosity of spirit—are still to be found in particular contexts (liberal helpings, liberal arts, liberal education).

Here in the United States, there has been a noble tradition of intellectual liberalism. John F. Kennedy, in his essay on the subject, said it wasn't so much a platform as an attitude of mind and of heart. Despite this, it is hard to exaggerate the animus that can be instilled into the word by conservatives. The term is often used as a synonym for radical, which is odd because liberalism has always been associated with gradualist reform, a process that exploits the existing machinery rather than sweeping it aside.

In the demonology of the right, liberals are sentimental self-deceivers, keen on federal as opposed to local government, reckless with the taxpayers' dollars and hell-bent on giving away the American dream to dodgy minorities like gays, Hispanics, godless pornographers, gun control campaigners, pregnant teenagers, environmentalists, and so on. In foreign policy, liberals are even more dangerous. The argument goes like this: liberals may be sincere, but they have a soft view of human nature that makes them reluctant to use force, an inhibition not shared by America's enemies who, heaven help us, are legion. Liberals undermine the country and all the rugged values that made it great.

The label is now burdened with so much freight that debates between liberals and conservatives often consist of each side imputing some absurd position to the other and then tilting at it.

liberty (n.) A glorious hurrah word. See **freedom**.

Local Resource and Archive Centre (np.) Also known as a Community Information Hub or an Ideas Store. This is a library with a DVD lending service, computers, and a notice board.

majority (n.) The majority, the vast majority, most reasonable people, the silent majority… These are all expressions whereby someone emphatic in a studio purports to be articulating a view on behalf of most of us. "Majority" has a mathematical meaning that every few years is tested by elections. Otherwise, the word should be used with care. Even if we agree with the opinion expressed (indeed, especially if we agree), we should question whether there would be a majority. "The man in the street" could be you, and the next man could be your maverick old pal whose every view is inimical to yours.

materialistic (adj.) Materialism is a philosophical doctrine asserting that only matter exists and that a physical connection must obtain between cause and effect. The popular meaning has to do with our preoccupation with stuff that, by implication, enfeebles our appreciation of the spiritual. If we are awash with cars, refrigerators, and huge color televisions, we are said by a disapproving pundit to be materialistic—or, by an approving one, prosperous. Clever advertising men do their best to persuade us that accumulating the latest toys will bring fulfillment, self-esteem, and irresistible sexual magnetism.

Emerging superpowers like China and India are rightly irritated when westerners, having enjoyed their own debauch, wag their fingers and warn against materialism. "First give up your gas-guzzling SUVs the size of cathedrals" might be their just response. The word "materialism" is sometimes used interchangeably with "consumerism" (see **consumer**): both are so broad that they hit many targets but do none of them a mischief.

Our appetite for things that make life comfortable and confer status seems to be hard-wired. Sneering only makes us resentful. With millions of years of evolution in one corner and a rational assessment of the state of the world in the other, the conflict looks like being a knockout in round one. We may be the first species to understand the means of our own extinction and be just too selfish to do anything about it. See also **-ism**.

militant (n.) Somebody who bothers to turn up. See also **activist**.

mistakes (n.) These are always made anonymously, in the passive and in the past. "Mistakes were made..." We all make mistakes. They are accidental and thus forgivable. By way of distinction, we add the qualifier "deliberate" if they are otherwise. But a politician caught up to his armpits in bribes, or some despot who "disappeared" his opponents, did not make *mistakes*. Their actions were intentional.

monitor (v.) "We will monitor this issue..." means doing nothing except watch TV and read the papers. "Carefully monitor" could mean a civil servant or a press clipping service keeps an eye out for it, but probably not. "Maintaining a watching brief" is another spuriously positive way of doing nothing.

more research needs to be done…(expression of piety) Of course it does. It would be a brave man who said "No, actually enough research has been conducted already." "More research" is a way of hedging. It says we haven't a clue what to do, but we are *concerned.*

Complex social problems benefit the educated middle classes (or a small subset of them, anyway). Solvent sniffing in Baltimore? Teenage delinquency in Cleveland? Better give the distinguished academic, Professor Serious, a substantial grant and ask her to do a study. Then if some journalist asks the minister or secretary what he's doing about it, he can say that he has appointed a high-powered team under Professor Serious who will be reporting to him as a matter of urgency. With more information, policy can be fine-tuned. That's so much better politically than saying "I don't know." In fairness to politicians, there are problems stemming from human nature that governments cannot do anything about—but that is not something we want to hear.

move on (cliché and v.) "We must move on…" is an expression uttered in tones of heroically suppressed irritation. The silly old public bangs on about our past delinquencies when the Promised Land lies in the future. Translation: forget everything, elect us again.

multicultural (adj.) A relatively recent hurrah word. Can we not only tolerate but celebrate our variety? However, we must face the fact there are people who don't want to live in a multicultural society. They yearn for the old, homogeneous one they grew up with. Multiculturalism is sometimes described as the tossed-salad model of society (delicious, but full of separate, spicy ingredients). It was not always so. A generation ago we boasted that America was a "melting pot" and were proud of the speed with which immigrant groups were assimilated.

The word also carries with it a sense that it may be myopic or even racist (see **racism**) to disparage the conventions of one culture from within the smug confines of another. This idea has a point, but the risk is that out of callow relativism we disqualify ourselves from making judgments about some fairly disgusting practices. Not all cultures are equally attractive, and not allowing ourselves to discriminate carries a high cost. The English used to decapitate miscreants—sometimes members of the royal family—in public. It was a smashing day out for the kids. It was part of the **culture**.

narrative (n.) We all have one now, even nations. The word has tunneled out of academia and into political jargon. Unlike history, a narrative can be fiction or nonfiction. How do you assess a narrative? Craft? Nifty construction? Textual analysis? Does it matter if it's true? See also **story**.

no plans at this time... (evasive phrase) A lie. Of course we have plans, but we don't want to admit to them. "At this time" or, portentously, "at this moment in time," or even such nuggets of bullshit as "within the current planning horizon" all serve as escape routes when the plan is announced shortly after an election.

old-fashioned conversation (euphemism) Though this is usually innocent, in some contexts it is understood to mean a bribe. It is obscure enough that whoever utters the expression—knowing the subtext will be understood—can preserve deniability.

on message (code) Doing what you are told. One day there will be advancement in all that abject toadying.

operational difficulties (np.) Railways, airlines, government departments: all suffer operational difficulties from time to time. What are they? Anything. Not bullshit exactly, but spray-gun words that cover everything in sight.

out of context (phrase) What a politician says when caught by the media saying something unpopular, stupid, or inconsistent with party policy. "I was quoted out of context." Who cares enough to check the context? Nobody. Besides, politics runs on mass amnesia.

oversight (n.) Lexicographers must be thrilled with this word, for it has changed its meaning in less than a decade. It used to be an inadvertent sin of omission, but then (presumably because it borrowed some of the meaning of "oversee") it elided into something more like supervision, of which etymologically it is a less Latinate version. In the Quaker religion it always had that secondary meaning because overseers have a pastoral role with the congregation.

You no longer commit an oversight (and grovel apologetically). You have oversight of an issue.

passion (n.) A hurrah word. People going into politics may start with passion, but it is soon drained from them after a few years in the business. They will still claim it, but only after an exacting calculation of the advantages.

perfectly clear (cliché) "I have made my position perfectly clear..." Actually, I obfuscated madly, and because—despite my mastery of bullshit—you understood enough not to like it, I am unwilling to repeat myself. "I have nothing to add" (to my statement of three weeks ago last Thursday) serves a similar function.

pledge (n.) A solemn promise, though the latent meaning (suggesting that something of value like a soul or a gold bar is left as surety) has been rinsed away by repetition. Nothing is forfeit now when pledges are broken. The word has a slightly archaic and traditional ring, lending a hint of religiosity to its use in the Pledge of Allegiance that school kids are expected to utter every morning. This practice—though voluntary—exerts a lot of peer pressure on youngsters and is controversial to the extent that the wording "one Nation under God" appears to violate the principle of the separation of church and state.

presentation (n.) An innocuous word that becomes burdened with Bullshit in one specific context. Politicians—especially if they pretend to be "conviction" politicians—rarely admit that they are wrong. But faced with a storm of excoriation for some particular idea, they can hardly pretend not to notice. Of course, they do not blame the silly old public for misunderstanding (God knows, they'd like to), and they are equally unable to concede that the public may have grasped the point only too well. Self-evidently, any policy of theirs must be sound. The best alternative is to see the problem as a purely technical one: the *presentation* must have been faulty.

proletariat (n.) The working class with a Marxist flavor. Even the most involuted social theories fail to describe adequately the mind-boggling complexity of society itself. Words steeped in theory are fine as long as the user makes the theory explicit. The danger is that the theory provides a kind of dictionary of objects that we can perceive and that anything not in the book will be squeezed until it fits the existing definitions. We seem to have a need for formalisms to help us make sense of the world. To some extent, they are all Bullshit.

public inquiry (np.) Politicians resist doing anything at all under public scrutiny if they can, but if pushed to the wall they will sometimes be forced to agree to a public inquiry. This is a time-honored device for taking the heat out of a scandal because it quickly becomes boring for the media, which tend to struggle with processes rather than events.

However, an inquiry runs the risk of keeping alive issues that a politician wants buried, so a report commissioned from some worthy like a judge or senior civil servant is preferable. (See **safe pair of hands**.) It stands to reason that the government should never hold an inquiry unless it is sure of the outcome. However, even if the inquiry is held in public, it still offers one benefit: it must be rigorous, and thereby it proceeds at a pace that makes continental drift look frisky. A trained legal brain following a paper trail can be so tedious that even a motivated observer will nod off.

No politician need answer any questions from the media on the subject of the inquiry—with luck for years. Naturally it would be wrong for him or her to anticipate and/or prejudice the findings. Another subtlety is that the government can define the remit of the inquiry so narrowly that not the slightest bat-squeak of political damage will ever be audible. If by mischance some shrill little fart of potential embarrassment still squeezes through the airtight gaskets, then the government has one last ploy; it can arrange for publication at the least opportune moment for media coverage. Friday evenings, too late for the TV news, are good. Selective leaks can also take the sting out of the report itself. The leaks can be dismissed as not worthy of comment, but when published, the report itself will have had its thunder stolen.

An investigation conducted in private is even better. Its report can be published very quietly—preferably long after the fuss has dwindled to nothing. A congressional inquiry, being televised, is more dangerous.

quality time (np.) Originally lifted from sociology, this expression was disseminated by journalists in the 1980s and 90s. People were working like rats in some horrible stress experiment and had little time for their children or spouse. However, with suitable planning, they could schedule "quality time." You could tell your kids that you had scheduled a "window" for some particularly satisfying interaction with them.

[a] question of semantics (all-purpose answer) This always sounds intelligent and is often true, or can be made to appear that way to a trained mind.

racism (n.) A predilection for making assumptions about human beings on the basis of their color. (See also **race**.) As a reason for imputing to someone a range of complicated human characteristics, the melanin content of his or her epidermis is manifestly stupid, and it is just as daft to disqualify yourself from making judgments on the same basis. The charge of racism is easy to make and it rightly carries a great deal of odium. It is tricky to refute. "I discriminate against him not because he is pink or brown, but because he is a bad man" can be a difficult message to put over in a society with an appetite for wickedness, a quality generally more thrilling than complexity. For this reason the term in some contexts can be seen as unfair, and this has enabled the word to be hijacked by the right. We are the wounded victims of a slander by the liberal establishment, they claim.

realistic (adj.) A popular word with many meanings. For instance, describing a settlement as "realistic" might suggest that it is the only one achievable. Alternatively, it is the best one having regard to all the constraints. ("We've faced the facts without flinching, taken them all into account, and we reckon that 5 percent makes sense all around…") In another sense, "realistic" is contrasted with idealistic; a realistic agreement is one rooted in practice rather than theory. "Realistic" can suggest that evidence has been collected in some hard-boiled fashion, in contrast to that of one's opponent who is dishonest or, more politely, mistaken. ("Our figures are realistic. His are fantasies plucked from his superheated brain…") By association, there is a subsidiary meaning of tough, maybe even a little courageous…

Realism in the political sense (for the word also has a specialized philosophical meaning to do with universals) is held to be a Good Thing. But all the multivalent meanings are deployed in a single word—one whereby a subjective judgment adopts a disguise and pretends to be a dispassionate description of the world. See also "the **fact** of the matter" and (under Corporate Bullshit) **the reality is…**

rendition (n.) Military euphemisms like "collateral damage" or oxymorons like "surgical strike" or "friendly fire" are so well rumbled that they are not worth fingering. However, recent events have furnished us with another term so bland that we could gulp it down without noticing how insidious it is. "Rendition" is used to describe the process whereby a prisoner being held in a U.S. base is lent to another regime to be tortured.

Soldiers seem to like that "-tion" suffix for turning verbs into nouns. "Pacification" (a notoriously brutal process) is one. "Interdiction" is another. "Interdiction of the enemy's infrastructure" means bombing the hell out of roads, bridges, pumping stations, and so on.

rights (n. – usually pl.) If only it were true, as the framers of the Constitution asserted so sonorously, that rights are inalienable. Given that several authors of that great document were slave owners, they must have had some caveats in mind from the beginning.

We like to think that we enjoy "human rights" by virtue of being born. This attractive idea is sustained only by our urge to believe it. The physical world does not confer rights on us just because we exist. Rights are legal entities and hence man-made. There are no property rights in **nature** (see New Age and Alternative Bullshit), for instance; look at predators around a kill on the African plain and see if you can spot any of them saying, "After you, old man…No, no, I insist. You were first." Perhaps hominids are different, more highly evolved? Alas, the evidence from primatologists about our genetic neighbors provides little comfort. Male gorillas commit infanticide to bring females back into estrus. Chimpanzees mount murderous raids on other groups even if there is more than enough food to go around. At least we humans have learned to govern our behavior by laws, however fallible. What's more, we enforce the rules with sanctions like fines, imprisonment—even death. This is protection of our own devising; there is none inherent in the human condition.

Rights granted by law to citizens (civil rights) differ between legal systems. In many parts of the world, if you are arrested, you do not have the right to call a lawyer, even if one were available. That would be a privilege that the policemen holding you might grant at their discretion after some merriment about your watching too much television. Such "rights" are not universal, but contingent on local legal codes, custom, and practice. That is why the rights we have embodied in law are so precious. The point is this: rights are changeable. Legislation, especially that passed quickly in a climate of fear, is nibbling away at our "rights" all the time.

Rights and the law are inextricably intertwined, and the law is something we have a duty to uphold. The law is drafted to prohibit unacceptable behavior, not to offer fulfillment. We do not have the right to go about our business unmolested, but anybody molesting us would be breaking the law. The distinction is important. We are protected from robbery, but not thereby granted a right to prosperity. That's something we must do for ourselves. Sometimes people confuse these ideas and become unhappy, querulous—even criminal—when they think that they have been dealt a bad hand and somehow cheated of their rights.

In the context of foreign policy, a reference to human rights indicates a regime which treats its own citizens badly. The twenty-first century dawned with a dismally large crop of such states still in place. Other governments deal with them, as they always have, with a mixture of hypocrisy, venality, and self-interest.

The language of human rights lays claim to a grandiloquent principle that sounds both fundamental and universal, but we should face it: we are not a nice species. Human rights violation may be cited as a reason to go to war against another country. History tells us that such interventions are rarely driven by nobility. We should listen carefully when some mover and shaker invokes human rights in order to justify a military adventure—especially if he's someone who usually cannot muster enough imaginative sympathy to care about the man next door.

road map (n.) A plan, but a little more vague. See also vision under Corporate Bullshit. In politics, a road map is a big plan in which certain things are supposed to happen in the right order for the next step to be taken. The road map may embody some general principles so it can be helpfully ambiguous. A map will allow for some diversion. After a negotiation with a long and painful history, woolliness can sometimes enable both parties to claim within their own constituencies that they have achieved some success. Clarity is not always an advantage. "Road map" is an old word in a new context, and usually only bullshitty when used to make a rather small plan sound grand. "Bridge building" and "road mapping" are often to be found in job ads for social workers.

robust (adj.) There have been negotiations when the participants loathed each other so intensely that they had to be physically separated while emollient diplomats shuttled between them. Riot police were once summoned to the Japanese Diet. Such discussions are always described as robust. See also **full and frank**.

roll out (v. and n.) Make some insipid little measure sound as inexorable as a tank.

safe pair of hands (coded np.) Someone with power, who will conduct an inquiry with a fine understanding of the ramifications of this and the complexities of that. In the final report nobody is to blame, but a long list of procedural recommendations reassures the public—if anybody still cares by the time the inquiry is concluded—that a first-class mind has been on the case. People with "a safe pair of hands" are smart, but deeply part of the culture they are investigating. Often they display a tenacious grasp of the minute particulars, and none at all of questions outside their terms of reference. Invariably, the latter are the ones the public wants answered. See **public inquiry**.

social exclusion (political code) The socially excluded are the poor. Sometimes also code for young black men. Also "socially disadvantaged"—the poor with grim backgrounds. Sometimes also a euphemism for the poor and not very bright. (The rich and stupid are not so much a problem as an opportunity.) A power base would not be worth a moment's purchase if a politician were to talk in such explicit terms.

solution (n.) A minor hurrah word. Chess problems can be solved because they are governed by formal rules. In the messy world, things can rarely be definitively solved. "Solution" is appealing and optimistic, for by definition it is the answer to a problem, even one that had not been perceived as a problem until that moment. The word is now found in all kinds of peculiar contexts (a "packaging solution," a "kitchen solution"?).

sophisticated (adj.), **sophistication** (n.) These are interesting. What do we imagine when we hear them? Clever metropolitan women, complete with cleavage and less-than-innocent smiles, exchanging wickedly inexplicit understandings with witty men in dinner jackets? Arguably sophistication is a kind of louche knowingness, not all that attractive. Historically the word had a pejorative meaning suggesting adulteration or falsity, but in general, now it has acquired a positive connotation.

The latter is what is exploited in expressions like "sophisticated system." This may be a euphemism for complex and costly. In Washington, a sophisticated system may be arcane to the uninitiated and thus able to do something to which the people in power would prefer not to admit. Who is excluded by a sophisticated vetting procedure, for example?

In the world of computer technology, "sophisticated" has a more cynical connotation. Sophisticated systems are designed to do everything the user could ever possibly wish to do, no matter how remote the contingency. The result is that they are catastrophically over-elaborate for the routine things that the user does 99 percent of the time. Why, you ask, are they made that way? There is one overwhelming reason: the marketing people want to sell an upgrade and have bullied the engineers into adding a host of features that make the overall architecture of the software warp like a bulkhead under pressure.

The words are even creepier in the context of ordnance. Nobody makes a gun or a missile anymore. The arms manufacturers produce "systems," invariably sophisticated ones. These are technically complex, are hugely expensive, and often don't work as intended. Men who like technology thrill to their specifications. Those on the receiving end will have the compensation of knowing that they have been reduced to gobbets of flesh by a sophisticated weapons system and not some crude iron bomb. See also **system**.

sources close to (political code) "Sources close to the White House…" means a press officer who, with the blessing of the boss, conveys information on the understanding that it is unattributable. In other words, it is something the powers-that-be wish to publish, though they would appear too self-serving or spiteful if their names were attached to it. Sometimes it is a matter of telling a reporter how to perceive an event in a way that is favorable. Occasionally words will be dropped "off the record" by the politicians to journalists who can be relied upon to play the game.

"Sources close to…" should not be confused with a deliberate leak which, in the Zen terminology, is an official leak. That's called "briefing against" some rival by dipping him in poison. An unofficial leak, on the other hand, is a heinous crime committed by a junior who must be ferreted out by the secret service and prosecuted with rigor.

spinmeister (n.) An honorary title roughly equivalent to a Doctorate in Bullshit (BsD).

statistics (n.) See Crapmatics.

story (n.) Journalists distance themselves from the emotional content of their daily toil on the grounds that everything that happens is just another story. The word has snuck into social work and is making an appearance in political rhetoric. Asylum seekers have stories, not biographies. In ordinary parlance a story may or may not be factual. It's as if it doesn't matter whether something actually happened or not; let's just see if the text delivers the goods. See also **narrative**.

subject matter expert (n.) "Subject" and "matter" are grace notes. See **expert**.

subsidiarity (n.) A deeply obscure concept from the European Union. It refers to the notion that political decisions should be taken at the lowest appropriate level, i.e., a local one if possible. Nobody understands how this works in practice, but it is a muscular word to invoke when countering anti-European sentiment from those who think that Brussels will take over their lives.

sustained funding stream (np.) Next year's money.

system (n.) Often an inchoate mess inhabited by the bewildered.

targets (n. and political fetish) In most contexts targets are fine, a definable goal, but they are only one, often misleading, aspect of the story. Targets are about numbers, and our response to numbers is almost superstitious. They represent hard information. Never mind the untested assumptions, the dodgy sampling procedures, the double counting, and so on (see Crapmatics). If one social worker helps a hundred families, that must be better than another who has only assisted five, even if the first one handed out a hundred leaflets and the second saved some lives. Numbers are abstract, an elegant symbol system that we find fantastically useful. But a cat does not have the quality of "oneness"—it's a cat. We have to be careful not to confuse the apparent precision of our numerical notation with the complexity of the world. See also **league tables**, Crapmatics, and **numerology** under New Age and Alternative Bullshit.

Because many people's brains experience a sudden panic in the face of large numbers, politicians find targets a seductive vehicle for obfuscation.

taskforce (n.) Forget fast cars and chunky chaps in body armor—in politics a taskforce is either a committee of civil servants or a quango (a quasi-autonomous non-governmental organization) of the well-paid good and great. Taskforces draft in people (always **experts**) at eye-watering expense because of their specialist knowledge. Within the military it is a unit, formed in response to media pressure, that enables those in power to look gritty and virile when questioned. It may even be an existing team expediently relabeled. The military taskforce will draw its members from the existing establishment and be quietly disbanded when the headlines recede.

tax (n.) Nobody likes paying taxes, but in an attempt to soften the blow, the government seems determined never to use the word without some favorable noun in apposition. Hence "tax revenue" and "tax investment."

tradition (hurrah word) Politicians who would not dream of being caught saying "We've always done it this way so that's how it must be done" are happy to deploy this word. It enjoys many positive connotations. Traditional values are thought to be moral, tolerant, and civilized; Victorian values are especially well regarded. Social historians of the period, however, also tell us about child prostitution, violence, crippling poverty, stultifying snobbery, obscene inequalities of opportunity, massive consumption of opiates, and savage exploitation of the workforce, including children. Bellicose empire building exported these practices to large areas of the planet.

triangulation (n.) It is tricky to work out what this new coinage is supposed to mean. First rising to prominence in the Clinton camp in the 1990s, context suggests that it is a new term for the process whereby one party attempts to occupy the traditional ground of another. If you risk saying "triangulation," look utterly confident.

tsar (n.) The head of any high-profile **taskforce**. If it is not high profile, he or she is the Chair.

under review (adv. phrase) We are doing nothing. See also **monitor**.

war (n.) War is a uniquely horrible human achievement often invoked as a metaphor for lesser conflicts. The war on drugs, the war on poverty, the war on supermarket trolleys… War is total, a convulsion affecting us all. It sounds so much more determined and dramatic than the mere announcement of a series of measures. But would that get the headlines?

Actual war used to be a conflict between states, an all-embracing upheaval affecting whole societies. For that reason it is difficult, not to say treacherous, to question the rightness of it when one's country is caught up in such a terrible spasm. That inhibition about showing disloyalty lingers on, to be exploited by the linguistically knowing when they use the word "war" in some lesser context. But in the twenty-first century, the old Diplomacy board of the Great Game has changed utterly. Now the strategists talk about "asymmetric conflict," for example between a superpower and a terrorist group. We need to discourage those in government from reaching for the manipulative word "war" when referring to some vicious local wrangle.

we/us/our (first person pl. parts of speech) Of course such vital little words cannot be bullshit, but note how often a politician will say "we" in a speech. There are two things at work. First, he or she is claiming membership of the great **community** that embraces us all. "Hey, we're all in this together" is the not-so-submerged subtext. In an age of political dynasties, cynics might argue that "they" and "we" have qualitatively different experiences of society.

The other function of "we" is sneakier, and it entails what linguists call a pronoun shift. Somebody will ask the politician for an account of his or her personal belief. "What do *you* think about this?" "*Our* position," replies the suit, sidestepping deftly, "is that *we* are concerned…"

while not wishing to (phrase) While not wishing to, say, suggest that my opponent is a prurient, scandal-mongering nutcase means the opposite: that is what I wish.

World Bank (n.) This immensely powerful organization is an adjunct of U.S. foreign policy. It tends to invest in capital projects (dams are a favorite) that are environmentally damaging and hard to maintain in the absence of much technical support. Corrupt national kleptocracies and dodgy American corporations reap the benefit. The policies imposed on poor countries by the World Bank as a condition for a loan are often economically catastrophic. Free trade allows in a flood of cheap produce that undermines local industries, especially agriculture. Poor countries may find their exports—cotton, for example—blocked by a bewildering quota system or simply unable to compete with heavily subsidized First World produce.

PART THREE

Crapmatics:
The Magic of Numbers

Some of you will have happened to run into
mathematicians and wondered how they got that way.

—Tom Lehrer

Mathematics is a complex and creative ability, akin to music. It enables us to think in ways not accessible to our everyday intuition and to speculate about the nature of things we will never be able to visualize. Without mathematics, science would be impossible. In the secret cabals and seedy bars where mathematicians meet, a great debate has rumbled on for centuries about whether the subject is invented or discovered. In other words, is it generated by the beauty of the notation and the ingenuity of man, or does it reflect the hidden, deep structure of the world? Some theorists believe that there is a sense in which the universe is just information and that mathematics is its organizing principle.

Happily, most of us never need worry about such migraine-inducing problems of mathematics. We cope from day to day with its nitwit younger brother—arithmetic. Now this *is* a language, one with a fierce and unbending grammar specifying what can and cannot be done within the rules. Just as English can be used for propositions that accurately describe the world ("the seventy-three bus runs past my door") or—just as grammatically—employed to utter statements that do not ("my purple armadillo lost his credit card on that bus"), the same holds for numbers. Two eggs and two eggs make four eggs because that is built into the meanings of two and four. However, you will never find all the decimal places of π or the square root of two in your kitchen, or, for that matter, anywhere else in the universe. In the language of numbers, both values run to an infinite sequence.[1]

Numbers borrow the cool mantle of mathematics. We imagine they are abstract and true by virtue of their consistency. Measurement may lie, we think, because it is carried out by shifty human beings, but the numbers themselves are inviolable. In fact, people who speak Number fluently can

[1] Pi has been calculated to over ten billion decimal places now, and still no pattern has emerged. You have to admire our perseverance.

con the rest of us all too easily, for our response to figures is that they represent hard information. Quantification is a vessel for an astonishing pitch and volume of Bullshit.

In the U.S., we seem to be particularly vulnerable to obfuscation by number. Despite efforts at reform, our education system still forces youngsters to specialize narrowly at an age when math may seem dauntingly difficult. What's worse is that we suffer from a kind of (let's hope) fading snobbery which rewards people who can chat about Florentine art on public service TV and undervalues those nerdy types who have the slightest idea of how the TV works. With patronizing grins we chortle about a dwindling handful of rainforest tribes, cherished by anthropologists, who count 1, 2, 3, 4, 5…umm…lots. However, it's not that uncommon to hear news broadcasts in which the news reader, probably with a major in English Literature, confuses millions and billions—a colossal three-orders-of-magnitude error. After all, the numbers are *damn big* and make little appeal to the imagination.

There are many species of mendacious numerical Bullshit. This chapter illustrates a few of the more common varieties.[2]

Average, mean, and median (n. and adj.) Suppose you work for a publisher on top of one of those slab-sided modern blocks for which the architect's inspiration must have been a large packet of cornflakes. There's tremendous excitement: Microsoft's Bill Gates has written a book (he did in fact, and gave the advance to charity). He will be visiting the office to chat with his editor about the pleasures of the semicolon.

[2]There are many good books on this subject, but I recommend for their accessibility the following: *A Mathematician Reads the Newspaper* by John Allen Paulos (Basic Books, 1995), *Imagining Numbers* by Barry Mazur (Farrar, Straus and Giroux, 2002), and *How to Lie with Statistics* by Darrell Huff (W.W. Norton, 1954). *The Sizesaurus* by Stephen Strauss (Kodansha Amer Inc., 1995) is also helpful for conveying an intuitive sense of large numbers. Huff's book is just as fresh today as when it was first published.

Bill arrives, and goes up in the elevator (for this is New York) with nine employees of the publishing house who each earn between $20,000 and $30,000 per year. Bill's annual income, for the sake of illustration, is $100 million.

The average or mean income for those in the elevator is just over $10 million each. Assuming the salary cost of the nine people other than Bill comes to a total of $250,000, the average is $10,025,000. This is derived by adding all the incomes and dividing by ten, the number in the group.

The median is $25,000. At this level half the inhabitants of the lift earn more and half earn less.

The *modal* value, however, is $27,380. By chance four of those in the lift are junior editors earning much the same, so most of the figures in the series cluster around this value. Sometimes a modal value is given as an "average." In this admittedly artificial example, the difference between the two "averages" is colossal.

Of course the profile of this elevator population is skewed by the presence of a billionaire, but the general idea holds good. If it had not been Bill in that elevator but the grossly overpaid CEO, he or she would still be able to boast that the "average" wage was pretty good.

You can do the same trick with property prices and thereby overstate the apparent value of houses in an area (maybe one of them is a palace) or understate the value (when talking to the local tax authorities, perhaps) if the number of cheaper houses happens to be a large proportion of the sample. God forbid, you might be tempted to adjust the boundary of your sample area to contrive that very effect.

Waiting times for hospital operations have even more variables. Unless it's printed with a large warning, the word "average" should be deleted from future editions of dictionaries.

coincidence (n.) No dark forces, no mysterious societies exchanging understandings in damp bunkers, no Priory of Scion, no silenced Black Helicopters, no alien pod thing sitting in the basement of Goldman Sachs, no strange geometries linking the great pyramids, Rennes-le-Château, and President Bush's left testicle…It's a big world with a lot going on and a population of 6.4 billion people and rising. Some will have dreamed about a lost pal the very night before he rings—or dies—but billions won't have. So what? Coincidences happen.

conditional probability (np.) The probability that Premier League soccer players will be rich is high. However, the probability that rich people will be soccer players is low. A may imply B, but that does not mean that B implies A.

Tabloid papers often confuse what mathematicians call conditional probability for mischievous effect. The probability that asylum seekers will need help from the state is high, but the probability that those seeking help from the state are asylum seekers is low. In fact, evidence suggests that the chronically unemployed are home-grown and/or from areas where some traditional industry has died. Asylum seekers, on the other hand, tend to take any job going.

Misunderstanding probability in court can have desperate consequences. A tiny fragment of DNA may contain a sequence found in only one in a million of the population. Does that mean that the man in the dock who has that DNA is overwhelmingly likely to be guilty? It may look that way, but the prosecution ought also to make another calculation. If one in a million carry that marker, then possibly nine people in a city the size of London could also carry it. Have they been eliminated? If not, there is room for reasonable doubt. The purely numerical argument must be supplemented by other evidence.

There have been a number of court cases in the UK involving women, each of whom tragically lost more than one baby through crib death. A forensic witness estimated the odds against such a tragedy striking the same woman twice or even three times by taking the normal distribution of such disasters per one thousand live births and multiplying the statistical probability by each heartbreaking repetition. The result came out as odds of millions to one, and the women were convicted of infanticide. But, with a UK population of over 60 million, more than 30 million will be female and nearly half of those will be women of child-bearing age. On this scale, such cruel coincidences could be expected to occur regularly over a period of years. The women in question were eventually acquitted. The court needed a statistician, not a medical expert. See also **coincidence** and **probability**.

correlation is not **causal** (phrase) We relish linear functions. They have an appealing simplicity and seem to make satisfying sense of the world. After all, we see them everywhere. The more we eat, the fatter we become. The further we drive, the more fuel we buy for the car.

Mathematicians talk about "mapping" one function onto another and look to see how close a fit can be achieved. But even if the fit looks perfect, it does not mean that the two functions are causally linked. There might be a very good match, for instance, between the increased consumption of ice cream and the incidence of pregnancy. The imagination starts back appalled at the vision of a nation licking vanilla off each other's bits. In fact it could be coincidence, or perhaps two functions correlate with a third. The arrival of summer, for instance? The start of the holidays? A scare about thrombosis and the Pill leading to less contraception and more comfort food?

An article in the *New Scientist* (March 2005) about a possible link between cannabis smoking in the young and psychosis illustrated the problem well. Is there a genetic disposition towards psychosis that also predisposes people to cannabis? Do people with psychosis self-medicate by taking cannabis? Do cannabis users move in circles in which other, more dangerous psychotropic drugs are available? Isolating some genuinely causal factor from the background takes large, well-designed studies and very careful analysis.

The danger of correlation appearing to be causal is more insidious if the relationship coincides with some prejudice. Suppose scruffy teenagers move into a home for delinquents and the nearby burglary rate goes up. Then the local paper publishes a graph showing the upward blip in crime that followed the arrival of said delinquents. Many of us would not need much persuading to connect the two events. But that would be a duff inference. Medieval scholastics recognized the flawed reasoning with the Latin tag *post hoc ergo propter hoc*. (Roughly, if it follows something it is because of it.) Actually, it may be that the notorious recidivist Mr. Mega Tea-Leaf got out of jail the very day the home opened, or the effect could be statistical noise, vanishing when looked at on a longer time scale.

All these difficulties are what statisticians call *confounding factors*. John Allen Paulos in *A Mathematician Reads the Newspaper* dramatizes this idea with a nifty example: the correlation between children's arm length and intelligence. (Both increase with age.) Here's that ice cream example in graphical form.

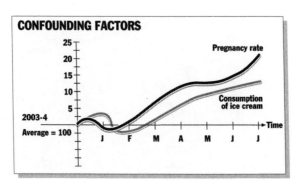

A correlation may be suggestive (and, God knows, will suffice for the tabloid press), but it is just not good enough evidence on its own to establish a causal link. See also **risk**.

graphs (n.) "Trace with graphs the bosom of the Pope" was an exam question in the renowned historical spoof *1066 and All That* by Sellar and Yeatman. Most of us find numerical information easier to grasp when it is translated into the form of graphs, pie charts, and other visual aids.

But graphs can be sneaky. In their simplest form, they relate two variables on a coordinate system. The position on a vertical axis represents one variable (the Stock Exchange index, for example) and the horizontal axis shows the other (like the chronology). At a glance you can see the movement over time. But consider the following three graphs.

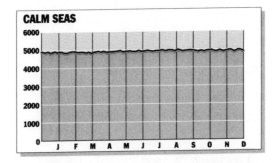

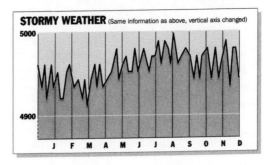

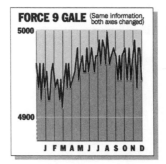

By adjusting the scale on the vertical axis, small changes look like a cross section of the Alps. Brokers might well be interested in these tiny movements, but to the rest of us, it looks stormy. Here the selection of the scale is misleading, and the same trick can be achieved by choosing just a little chunk of time. Consider the quite different effect of these two:

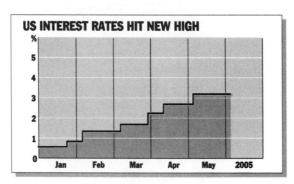

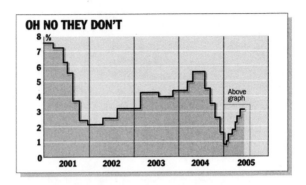

Another trick designed to make us smite our foreheads and gasp is to use a cute little drawing of the variable you are illustrating. Obesity in children has been in the news, so why not dramatize the graph with diagrammatic versions of kids? If the incidence has doubled, double the height on the vertical axis. Fair enough? But the volume of the schematic children has more than doubled; on a casual glance, the visual effect is more alarming. See the graph below.

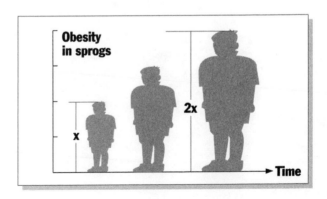

There's a similar visual trick with pie charts.

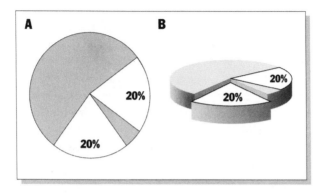

Perhaps most irritating of all is when the vertical axis is missing altogether, as below.

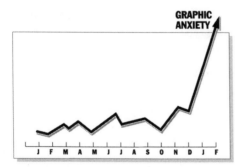

This could be measuring graph-induced anxiety. It could be anything.

group reassurance (np.) You can buy this product, and trust it, because everybody can't be wrong. Mind you, a cynic has pointed out that if you can fool all the people some of the time, that sure is long enough to be President of the United States.

81

Paradoxically, surveys used in advertising are both true and utterly dishonest. You want to say that 99 percent of people reported that your toothpaste enhanced their appeal to the opposite sex or that nine out of ten cats went nuts for your Moggiesplodge, spurning all rival products. Here's the trick: conduct lots of surveys. Throw away the ones that don't give you the result you want, and wait for the statistically anomalous one that finally comes up trumps. If challenged, you will be able to produce it.

Alternatively, just select the sample (which could be tiny) from respondents who you know already will produce the desired answer, and then word your claim carefully. Just say that 100 percent of the customers *you asked* (i.e., all five of them) reported that the Whizzo-Supamattress gave them better orgasms.

In the case of Moggiesplodge, this may just be sharp practice, but in other circumstances it is darker. Recent scandals published in the technical press revealed that pharmaceutical companies had been guilty of simply not publishing negative results of drug trials despite knowing full well that such data are scientifically important. Negative information is still information. Now the FDA (Food and Drug Administration) and other licensing authorities want to see all the research and not just a favorable selection.

incidence (n.), **absolute numbers** (np.) If you want to make a number sound big, you quote the total. Three hundred people in America have caught scrotum-eating Goolie Disease, screams *USA Today*, and there's no cure! Be appalled by terrible pics on pages three, five, six, and eleven! Alternatively, you can cite the incidence: your sensible *USA Today* tells you not to panic—only one in a million ever catch Goolie Disease. For a population of 300 million, both are true.

Remember that to multiply and divide big numbers, you can just add and subtract the exponents, the power to which the number has been raised. The U.S. population can be thought of as roughly 3×10^8. So if an earnest man on television makes an appeal on behalf of those suffering from Bullshitter's Syndrome (a compulsion to say "proactive" every second sentence) and maintains that as many as one in two hundred suffer from it, the quick way to calculate the total number of victims of this tragic condition is to think of 200 as 2×10^2. Then you subtract the exponents; eight minus two is six. So the answer will be a number that is ten to the sixth power, i.e., a million. This has dealt with the big number component. The little numbers are easy. Divide two into three; answer 1.5. The number of people with Bullshitter's Syndrome is therefore $1.5 \times 10^6 = 1.5$ million. The figure seems a little low for Bullshitter's Syndrome, but the technique is a handy way of getting a sense of the credibility of numbers.

Special interest groups tend to overclaim when quoting rates of incidence. Simple arithmetic will tell you how such rates translate into, say, real people. If the answer intuitively seems odd, perhaps it is wrong. For many reasons, relatively tiny figures sometimes receive great attention. Heroin overdoses, for example, kill a very small number of people compared to alcohol or road accidents, but they have a kind of sick glamour that chimes in with a societal preoccupation with illegal drugs.

The golden rule is this: it's always worth looking at the underlying numbers.

millions and **billions** (n.) A million is 10^6 (1,000,000) and a billion is 10^9 (1,000,000,000). The higher cognitive functions of otherwise really bright people are sometimes paralyzed by these big numbers, but they can easily be backed snarling into a corner.

Imagine you have a dripping bath tap. Every second a large drip of about half a cubic centimeter plops on to the plug that by mischance you have left in place. Do you think a million drips will fill the bath? Hmm. A million drips is half a million cubic centimeters or five hundred liters, half a cubic meter. You could buy five hundred one-liter bottles of mineral water and easily store them in your bathroom (but don't try it, as they will weigh half a metric ton). That would be enough to fill about three to four baths. At a drip per second, it would take about eleven and a half days to reach a million. A billion drips from the same tap would take nearly thirty-two years, weigh in at five hundred metric tons, and displace five hundred cubic meters, a smallish swimming pool.

Looking at it in reverse, one part per million is thus equivalent to a second in eleven and a half days and a part per billion is a second in thirty-two years. This is worth remembering now that analytic techniques like gas chromatography can detect concentrations down to parts per billion. Although there are substances that are dangerous even in such minute quantities, it raises the question of whether our anxieties about such issues as agricultural chemicals getting into the food chain have risen in proportion to the sensitivity of the detection apparatus (see **threshold** under Professional Bullshit).

These numbers may seem too huge to grasp, but they are not that large in the context of a big population or a government budget.

In the United States, with its population of about 300 million, a billion dollars represents an annual $3.33 per person, enough for a cheeseburger and fries maybe. The U.S. Congress has authorized a total defense budget of $419.3 billion for the fiscal year 2006. Now that is a genuinely frightening number (equivalent to about $65.50 for every human being on Earth or enough—at Afghan market prices—to buy every single one of us, not excluding babies, a Kalashnikov assault rifle). The sum is more than the next twenty big spenders combined.

normal (adj.) A word that may be handy in statistics, but is misleading in most other contexts. Nobody is quite sure, for instance, what a normal sex life might be. As the word cannot escape overtones of approval or disapproval, it's probably best melted down for scrap. That is not to say that anything goes, because it doesn't, but other moral principles (such as not hurting others) legislate more effectively against unacceptable behavior than invoking some idealized notion of normality.

numbering your points (np.) This can be a trick for sounding logical. What a cool, analytic intelligence is at work here, you think. Yet point five is a differently worded version of point one, and point six is actually incompatible with point two. George Carlin, the American comedian, has a list of reasons for doing something that goes as follows: 1, b, iii, four, e, vi.[3]

opinion polls (np.) Darrell Huff in *How to Lie with Statistics* posits sending out a survey that includes the question: How willing are you to fill in surveys? By definition 100 percent of the respondents would have been willing, thus prompting the headline result that a recent (they are always recent, aren't they?) survey reveals that everybody is willing to respond to surveys. Bullshit. And in a narrow sense it is true.

Pollsters cannot interview the entire population so they try to select a demographically balanced sample that reflects the makeup of the population as a whole. This is tricky. Imagine you are a pollster on a rainy street, and you're armed with lots of forms, a clipboard, and an aching smile. The profile of your interviewees should include six middle-class white people, two of whom must be females over forty. But assessing age can be fraught with difficulty. Better err on the side of caution and ask some obviously elderly women who are unambiguously over the age criterion. But do old ladies bias the result? You're also struggling to find two working-class males under twenty-five who won't tell you to bug off and three second-generation Asians. What's more, you're freezing your ass off. Better cheat.

The questionnaire is one of those tick-box jobs that can be easily coded and processed in a computer. But what happens on the windblown pavement? You ask someone if she would describe herself as "more satisfied," "less satisfied," "very much less satisfied," or "about the same" over the dustbin service. You get a rant about the folly of privatization. In fact your interviewee doesn't give a stuff about the dustbins, but despite not having an opinion she still has to select one from the range of options. She may be arbitrary or, despite her passion, go for the most neutral. If instead you conduct the survey by phone, that presupposes that everybody has a phone.

[3] Quoted by John Allen Paulos in *A Mathematician Reads the Newspaper* (1995)

What time of the day do you select to be sure of getting the respondents you need? Many of the people you should interview to achieve the right profile for the sample will be too tired to be willing to spend time talking, or perhaps they will be out. You haven't got their cell phone numbers.

All the attempts to cut corners by balancing the sample increase the margin of error. The most important factor is the size of the sample. A survey of ten thousand from a population of ten million will be more accurately predictive than a survey of ten from a population of ten thousand, even though the ratios between the sample size and the population will be the same.

In practice, there are many, many complexities. All polls have a margin of error. Sophisticated pollsters admit to a margin of error of 2 or 3 percent, though it's likely to be higher, as the Democratic Party found out to its despair following the Florida exit polls in the 2004 election. Publishing the poll before an election may in itself affect the result as it could depress or encourage one group or other, or lead others to adopt tactical voting. See also **spurious precision** and **group reassurance**.

percentages (n.) Percentages of what? A local paper in announced in huge type on its front page that rape in a small city (population c. 190,000) was up 60 percent. It was, but reading the text revealed that the number of incidents had increased from five to eight. It is a horrible crime, but the incidence is still fairly low. Headline writers like percentages because a change in a small sample translates into a frightening figure.

More irritating still are percentages of unspecified numbers. Twenty percent more! Fifteen percent less! Less than what? These numbers that float around, unconnected to anything, are bullshit.

A favorite advertising ploy is to express the value of whatever is being measured as an inverse percentage of the whole. Don't say "10 percent fat" (a real heart-stopper). Say instead "90 percent fat-free!"

probability (n.) A fearsome branch of mathematics put on a formal basis centuries ago by Pascal and Fermat, he of the infamous Last Theorem.

Probability is often cited as a fraction or a percentage. A one-in-five chance (or 20 percent probability) of dying in New York from being hit by a bus (this is an invented figure) may inhibit you from going anywhere near the place. What it does *not* mean is that when you visit New York, you have a one-in-five chance of being mown down by a double-decker. No, what it means is that of all the deaths recorded in New York, one in five will have been caused by buses. The probability is calculated from the small and unlucky subset of people who snuffed it; it is not a fraction of the hugely more numerous live population.

There was a scary story about breast cancer and HRT (hormone replacement therapy) that suggested that a woman is slightly more likely to suffer from breast cancer if she is taking HRT. The picture, however, is influenced by many factors such as age, family history, genetic predisposition, and even such subtleties as the fact that HRT seems to have some role in protecting against heart attacks—thus increasing the number of women in the HRT group who survive to contract cancer. Isolating just one variable takes extremely careful study. The task is made more difficult by the fact that the most rigorous scientific method, the double-blind trial in which neither the investigators nor the patients know in advance who is getting what, is morally impossible to carry out if people are dying.

I can only comment on how the figures were reported, and that was in a manner that almost certainly caused dismay to the painstaking epidemiologists who had done the work. A percentage increase looks alarming. For instance, a rise in incidence from 10 to 11 per 100 is a 1 percent increase, but a rather more frightening-looking 10 percent gain in probability.

Some probabilities change, and others don't, despite our conviction that they damn well ought to. The probability of finding an ace from a randomly shuffled pack of cards is one in thirteen, or 7.69 percent (fifty-two cards and four aces). As long as you discard the misses, the probability will improve with each try as the number of cards other than aces diminishes. But many other random processes (such as the lottery or tossing a coin) undergo no change in their probabilities no matter how many repetitions are performed. This seems counter-intuitive. If the odds are 50/50 or 1/2 that a coin will land heads, yet it consistently turns out to be tails, then the purely mathematical calculation of the probability of all those tails looks like it ought to be 1/2 x 1/2 x 1/2…and so on, with each flukish repetition becoming more improbable. The problem is that in the real world a flipped coin cannot "know" how it landed last time; any random sequence of coin tossing is likely to have many runs of the same result, only gradually regressing to the expected norm over a large number of iterations. You could keep the same lucky lottery numbers for a thousand years, and the odds against them coming up would still be exactly the same.

Such systems have no memory. Depressing, isn't it?

rounding (n.) The other side of the coin from **spurious precision**. We yearn for figures that can be grasped intuitively. "About a third…Nearly half…" Hmm. Because we have ten digits and a decimal system, we have a particular affection for numbers based on ten. "Three out of ten men once…Seven out ten women admit…" say the headline writers. Looks a bit glib, doesn't it? If our number system used base twelve, we'd probably focus on other numbers. "Oh woe, not another dozen," we'd moan on our thirty-sixth birthday.

Rounding can be useful. Human body temperature is 37° Celsius, a number established by the nineteenth-century German physician Carl Wunderlich, who averaged many readings and rounded them slightly. In Fahrenheit the equivalent is 98.6°. In fact, body temperature wobbles up and down on a diurnal cycle; a few tenths of a degree Fahrenheit is not significant and the greater precision of the Fahrenheit scale may have led to misplaced anxiety. The memorable centigrade number makes sense.

On the other hand, rounding applied to large populations represents significant errors. About one in ten in America, says that man in the suit emoting on TV, suffer from chronic Bullshitter's Syndrome and need our help. His (already fallible) survey gave him an actual figure of 8.9 percent. The fudge factor in this example would be 3.3 million people.

spurious precision (np.) It is impossible to devise a sample that precisely reflects a whole population. The only way of doing that is to survey everybody (a census), an exercise of great administrative complexity and expense. Addresses will be out of date; people will miss dates, mess up the forms, or deliberately falsify them. The most careful census will contain many inaccuracies. Even much smaller investigations always have a margin of error.

For instance, despite being designed to avoid cultural bias, IQ tests have margins of error. If some chap tests at 103 you think, hmm, just a smidge smarter than average. If another boy's score is 98, you might imagine he is just a tiny bit less bright than average. However, if the margin of error is 5 percent, you are really not entitled to make any inference at all. The man who scored lower may be more intelligent (leaving aside the question of what it is that IQ tests actually measure) than the one with the higher score.

I once worked for a publisher with a rather frightening sales director. When cornered, he would invent statistics. "I happen to have read the research," he would say in a confident regional accent, "and can tell you, sunshine, for a fact that 47.34 percent of all purchasers of romantic fiction are women called Margery in supermarkets south of the river Trent." We all suspected it was bullshit, but nobody dared question the precise figures.

In another company, costing was the god. It was as if the corporation was afraid of judgment, but trusted numbers. Assumptions were fed into a clever piece of software available online to all the so-called "fluffies" (the editorial types). Before you could mutter "viable," project costs were calculated to two decimal places. But those initial assumptions were often little better than guesses. The author may not have written the book at the time of acquisition so the extent, and thus the printing cost, were not precisely known. The selling price was also a guess, as was the rate of returns that would obtain when the book finally appeared. (Returns happen when the bookshops send back those books the fickle public has found it in its heart not to buy.) The costing included many other variables based on experienced guesswork.

The accuracy of the machinery disguises the sogginess of the assumptions. The result of that costing should have been expressed to plus or minus 10 percent—maybe more. Those decimal places were Bullshit.

A more important example of this phenomenon is the economic model, which, regardless of its level of complexity, is invariably wrong. Economies are the ultimate chaotic systems, exquisitely sensitive both to the starting conditions and to small perturbations.

We should scoff when some Treasury economist with a high forehead and a double major squints judiciously into the distance and makes a numerical prediction. If there's a decimal point in it, feel especially free to shout "Bullshit!" See also **rounding**.

standard deviation (statistical device) This is a handy concept with which to inoculate yourself against statistical bullshit.

Imagine—if you can—that you are a statistician. (The UK government's chief statistician once observed that he would have been an accountant, but he didn't have the charisma for it.) You are plotting a function with two variables—say pints of beer consumed and the age of the drinkers. All the numbers lie roughly along a line and you suspect they will peak with twenty-three-year-old males who drink far too much. You take the average of all the values you have collected and calculate a mean value for different ages of drinkers or—if you are displaying the figures on a graph—draw a line showing the change in beer drinking as age increases. The actual values will be distributed around the average and are unlikely to fall exactly on the line on your graph. After all, common sense tells you that no one boozer is likely to be Mr. Statistically Perfect.

To derive the standard deviation, you look at all the numerical differences between the measured values and the average, and multiply those differences by themselves, i.e., you square all the deviations. Then you average those squared numbers and calculate the square root of that new number. That's the standard deviation. It may sound a bit baroque, but if you stop to think it's a cleverly synoptic way of calculating the dispersion of values around a mean.

Life is never neat. A large standard deviation might suggest that some hypothesis you had about the relationship between the functions you were plotting may be imaginary. Your guess about the beer and the drinkers was plain wrong. For the rest of us, it's worth asking about the standard deviation. It gives the statisticians pause.

units (n.) Budgets are calibrated in currency. National budgets come in billions, often with some suspiciously synoptic categories (administration?). But politicians use strange units. Nuclear power stations, hospital beds, nurses, jet fighters, and babies have all been drafted in to make a polemical point about priorities.

For the cost of one F-22 Raptor (currently about $187 million), says a Member of Congress, the government could buy 340 CAT scanners. Then my constituent—Sweetly Smiling Little Old Lady X, a recent star of the popular press—would have been diagnosed in good time. Of course, the Congressman knows that with our structure of government, the likelihood of money passing from one place to another after the budgets have been allocated is about the same as finding the works of Proust in orbit around Pluto.

Different things cost different amounts of money. The government thinks we need them all. In order to make a number sound small, you compare it to something expensive and unattractive. This teeny-weeny grant to our theater company, the Strindberg Comedy Players, is life or death to us—but it would only buy half a gun mounting on a battlefield tank or fifteen inches of ear-shattering new runway.

Another common ploy is to boil the statistics down to units that we can easily imagine. Every two minutes, somebody in the world will contract AIDS! In Hackney, twenty teachers a day are attacked by pupils! These examples dramatize numbers and, with a hint of black humor, they sound as if the problem has been put on a grimly systematic basis. Another day has passed—better find some teachers to bash up (if that is what is meant by "attacked") to meet our quota. The figures are compiled by taking an annual **incidence**—something that is itself potentially misleading, as it puts highs and lows into the same pool for averaging—and dividing the resulting number into time. (In the case of the teachers, presumably it is the hours they are at school that determine the frequency.) The technique is simpleminded and often wrong—not necessarily on account of bad faith but simply because journalists and politicians are so poor at arithmetic.

There are 525,600 minutes in a year. For rough calculation, you can think of it as half a million, so that's the same number of people who will be affected annually by something happening to mankind at a rate of one per minute. It's approximately 1/13,000 of the number of human beings on Earth (the 2005 estimate is 6.4 billion) and far less than the annual increase in population. Always look at the underlying numbers when somebody chooses to represent figures this way.

yield (n.) Redolent of agriculture and finance, this term was first used by the military for the kilo- or megatonnage of nuclear weapons, and it has since spread. "Improving the yield" sounds so benign. "Payload" is the other word used in this context, and etymologically, it also contains some of the pleasurable connotations of money. Both are fine examples of how we use euphemism to describe the technology of killing each other.

PART FOUR

Sales and Marketing Bullshit:
Your Call Is Important to Us

The market is a place set apart where men may deceive each other.
—Anacharsis, Scythian philosopher, c. 600 BC

Selecting marketing words for inclusion in a Dictionary of Bullshit is a thankless task, for sales and marketing are all bullshit. But at least most of it is lowercase "b" bullshit. We enjoy the fact that some very inventive minds have been employed to persuade us that we cannot limp through life a moment longer without some gewgaw, and we appreciate their efforts.

The wit, the production values, and the sheer narrative compression achieved by TV ads, for instance, are breathtaking. Marketing is such clever bullshit that, by and large, we can only smile. What's more, it is pushing at a door already wide open. We want all this stuff, as well as the success, perfect thighs, sexiness, witty and affectionate family life, and all the other dreams that the marketing men have conditioned us to associate with it. Those selling it to us understand that our desire for it is not rational. The marketing men and women have a working knowledge of our unconscious desires that would delight a psychologist; they have linked the acquisition of stuff with our deepest needs and anxieties. Very few products (apart from computers, maybe) are sold on their specifications alone.

Our consumer economy depends on us buying ever more things. The fact that this debauch is unsustainable is not our problem. With any luck, the world will see us out.

architect-designed (real estate language) Nearly everything was designed once, even if it then became a template for endless repetitions. The question arises: was the architect any good? Sometimes the expression means white-painted, Zen, and minimalist—qualities that look great in photographs. People clutter up the effect badly.

awesome (adj.) Just one of many adjectives that have become so devalued by advertising copy that even such things as T-shirts can be awesome, or even, like, totally awesome.

bargain (n.) No, it's not, though we'll use our elbows to get to the front of the queue anyway.

because you deserve it… (copy line) This has many variants. You know you don't *need* this thing, and therefore you feel guilty about wanting it. The advertiser is giving you permission to have it. Damn it, you're wonderful and entitled to a treat. It is a brilliant line.

bestseller (n.), **bestselling** (adj.) Sometimes true, but often a status claimed for some unimpressive sales figures in the hope that the description will be self-fulfilling. Buy it because the whole world is buying it. You wouldn't want to be "sad."

butt brush (np.) A legendary discovery from the famous marketing guru Paco Underhill. If you make the aisles in a shop too narrow in order to maximize the space available for merchandise, sales may go down. This is because women do not like to stop and browse if other people, including men, have to squeeze past them, giving rise to the infamous "butt brush." This insight made Paco rich and persuaded many companies that marketing is clever stuff.

Buy now, pay nothing until… (promotional offer) A seduction for the feeble-minded. The cost to the retailer of the deferred cash is added to the price when the payment date comes around—as it will before you can say, "Oh dear, I'm over-extended."

Buy one, get one free (enduring sales pitch) Buy twice as many as you want at a price that still gives the retailer a profit, if only because the supplier has been bullied into finding the promotion. Also seen in the form of "two for the price of one."

carpet bombing (np.) Borrowed—with dubious taste—from warfare, "carpet bombing" became the term used by insiders to describe the endless flow of mail shots, unsolicited credit card offers, leaflets from pizza delivery services, brochures, and all the other volumes of stuff that is squeezed into our mailbox on a daily basis.

celebrity endorsement (np.) Intellectually, we know that we do not acquire the glamour of some film star by buying things that he or she has advertised. The appeal is unlikely to be the quality of the product itself; we are a cynical lot and understand that the celebrity has been paid huge wads to endorse it. So what is going on in our minds? Do we in some way identify with the person by acquiring the same stuff (even though we know that he or she almost certainly does not buy it in reality)? Can we imagine that by having this thing, we will become as admired and sexy as the celebrity? Is that why things worn on the body like sneakers, clothes, perfume, and watches are particular favorites for endorsement?

The technique obviously works. Hard-nosed companies and their advertising agencies toady for the privilege of pressing giant checks on to celebrities, most of whom already have a surplus of the folding stuff. See also **product placement**.

characterful (adj. used by estate agents) Really strange and inconvenient.

charming (adj.) Unbearably kitsch.

 Closing down sale! Everything must go (shop banner) Some retailers have been closing down for decades.

collectable (n. and adj.) You've got discrimination and are pretty shrewd with it. Other people accumulate trash, but you are a collector. And one day all your collectables may have increased in value. Pathetic how easily we are manipulated by a single word, isn't it? See also **connoisseur**.

computer (n.) See **Information Technology (IT) excuses**.

connoisseur (n.) This is what you will become if you buy the product. China bunnies, limited-edition gilded collectable serving plates, alloy replicas of World War II Spitfires, glass models of the Vatican complete with illuminated Pope—there is nothing so dire that some marketing man will not congratulate you for being a connoisseur when you hand over money for it.

craftsman-made (adj.) A boast in many a catalog. You may even have a picture of the craftsman, a smashing, nut-brown, gnarled old man with a leather apron and deep love for the texture of wood. But remember **just-in-time** (see Corporate Bullshit) inventory management. Your wooden DVD cabinet will not be made until you've placed your order. Forget gnarled old men; think machines—or vast factories in Chongqing.

credit (n.) If you have a platinum or gold card, a wallet full of other bits of plastic, and enough credit to buy a small country, snooty maître d's in pretentious restaurants are supposed to crash to their knees with involuntary orgasms and a cry of "Oh sir, that will do brilliantly. Let me polish your boots with the grease from my nose." Credit is desirable, and it's not surprising that the other meanings of the word are all positive. A generation ago it was called something else: debt.

critical mass (np.) Being big enough.

critical mass footfall (np.) Getting enough people into the shop.

customer service (np.) With a dwindling number of exceptions, companies lose interest after the sale. Nothing dramatizes this more than the anguish of the telephone call you attempt to make after the newly acquired dishwasher or computer has gone wrong.

The number to phone for customer service may well be on a premium line (a 1-900 prefix). This added cost is rarely, if ever, made explicit, so you will be ripped off both ways: on your phone bill as well as by the failure of your gadget. The call will lead you to an automated voice-management system ostensibly designed to direct you with maximum speed to the right department. In fact, while your telecom meter runs feverishly, the system will keep you on the line while it shuffles you through two or even three levels of choice, none of which quite fits your needs. When eventually you do select what you hope is an appropriate option, the phone will play you synthesized Mozart or—even worse—cover versions of rock and roll once performed by passionate musos and now relegated to music hell. Every two minutes, a centerfold automated voice will thank you for your patience and assure you that your call is important. "Aagh! Christ on a bike! I'm not patient," you yell, but in voice management space there is nobody to hear you scream. When, or if, you do eventually connect with a human being (and it's not unknown to be timed out after holding forever), you have to be scrupulously polite. You do not want to go through that again.

Some retailers have made this process so famously horrible that they offer an over-priced service guarantee that appears to bypass it. In fact you end up paying for—for the first year at least—what are rights freely granted under statutory consumer law. But perhaps the bespoke retailer's insurance protects you from inconvenience and dangerous surges in blood pressure? Alas, no. The small print specifies that you must use their engineers for any callout. These heroic men and women, living in a hormonal soup of intense public irritation, are in great demand. Unsurprisingly, they may be unable to get around to you for some time.

cutting edge (n. and adj.) Applied to technology (and borrowed from the military), this is praise from nerds. In the sense of innovative, it is usually a lie or deeply silly. Do we really need an electric pepper mill, a ballpoint pen that records memos, or a rattan garden pig?

demographics (n.) The geography of people. Often employed by marketers to impress clients with the idea that who buys what is a science.

 designer (n. and adj.) You can buy a pair of jeans in a supermarket for as little as $6, or you can pay twenty-five times that much for a "designer" pair. Both are manufactured in factories in the Far East—China, Indonesia,

Vietnam—by nimble-fingered women and girls working long hours on minimal wages. Possibly in the same factories. The difference between the jeans lies in the stitching over the pockets, possibly the weight of the cotton, and certainly the boost to the self-esteem of those who can afford the conspicuously expensive versions.

The value of designer names is such that they have expanded into other areas in a process known as brand extension. (See **brand** under Corporate Bullshit.) Hence we have Boss watches, Mont Blanc wallets, Porsche sunglasses. Hard-eyed marketing men with MBAs and careful haircuts have decided that names associated with luxury in one product can be "leveraged" to add value to another. You are paying for the name rather than the quality of the product.

Even underwear can now carry a designer label, and in response fashion has evolved the plumber's crack-revealing, low-slung baggy pants so that the logo can be displayed for the delight of passersby. Almost anything to adorn the body can now boast a smart name. In some cases the name itself (e.g., Tommy Hilfiger sweatshirts) is the design, surely the ultimate marketing trick.

Does this mean that some designer has created the template for every item? Or does the phenomenon owe more to the intellectual property lawyers than talented individuals? In fact, vast luxury goods houses license their designer brand names for commercial gain. Imagine them spieling to distributors at trade fairs: "Here's our special Gullible Range at four times the price…"

economy size (np. and adj.) Freaking huge. We assume that a truckload of laundry detergent is cheaper per pound than buying a mountain of small packets. It may be a bit, though not invariably, so it's worth doing the math to check. But you've just bought enough to do your laundry for a year, tied yourself to that product for all that time, and improved the manufacturer's cash flow.

There is a good ecological argument for reducing the volume of packaging, but in the West it is almost impossible to take your own container to a retailer for a volume or weight-based refill. The U.S., for example, generates 1,400 pounds of household waste per person per year.

economies of scale (np.) A sophisticated way of explaining a bargain. Our buying power, boasts the big chain, allows us to pass on to you, the **consumer** (see Political Bullshit), these economies of scale. Dimly we realize that the chains have screwed the suppliers into the ground and that we will be getting a mass-market product made by cheap labor. The logic of this is that eventually there will be a smallish number of enormous factories, probably visible from the moon.

exclusive (adj.) To whom? Obviously the manufacturer, as we cannot be so naïve as to imagine that a single one will be made just for us. If the design of the product deviates by an atom from the one produced by the rival manufacturers, then it can be advertised as exclusive. Even if it's identical, the manufacturer may still claim that it is the only model made by them—and thus exclusive.

Extra! (starburst on packets) Ten percent more—than what? The standard contents of the packet presumably. But should we presume? Maybe it's just a bigger packet. Regulation ensures there probably is 10 percent more than the usual packet (as if we were familiar with the contents of that down to the last gram), but it raises the question of why the manufacturer does not always give us that much. There is fierce competition; these regular come-ons help tie us to particular brands. It would be so much better for our poor planet if we could take our own containers to the stores and fill them with commodities ourselves. (See **economies of scale**.) Of course, that would not allow for all the marketing at the point of sale, as it is known in the jargon.

facilitator (n.) A man or woman with a confident and fluent manner who can organize a sales and marketing conference and charge several thousand dollars a day without laughing.

Fantastic savings! Up to 70 percent off... (promotional hype) There won't be many of those. Retailers are not dopes. They want to entice us into the stores so they put the biggest bargains in the window as a lure. The best discounts are for the slowest-moving items. That pullover in sphincter brown and staphylococcus yellow might not have moved for good reason.

happened to be in your area... (phrase) Our team of high-pressure salesmen happened to be in your area with a fantastic deal on vacuum cleaners and vinyl siding. Oh happy day!

incentives (n.) Prizes, money, or bribes. To "incentivise" is to offer such items.

Information Technology (IT) excuses (a field of study in itself) "I'm sorry, my screen's gone down. I'm sorry, I cannot do that from here—you will have to write. I'm sorry, the computer's rebooting—could you call back? I'm sorry, but I cannot remove your name from our database. I'm sorry, the inventory software said there was a part on the van—I'll just zip back to the depot. I'm sorry—the system will not let me transfer you to that department. I'm sorry. I'm sorry..."

infotainment (n.) Imagine the alarms going off at the script conference in the TV company making its umpteenth documentary about sharks, aliens, big weather, or volcanoes. Whoop, whoop! Fact warning. How the hell, you can imagine the script editor saying, did that sneak in? Better start rewording right away in case there's another one lurking downstream.

Infotainment purports to be educational, but it avoids any real information in favor of spectacular visuals. Every so often, a creamy voice-over will explain that nature is letting herself go in all her awful majesty.

Infotainment makes a lot of profit. The same archive of film can be permuted endlessly and the voice-over format means that the result can be sold all over the world with a local actor dubbing the commentary into the appropriate language. Parents in many countries subscribe to the channels that disseminate this stuff in the belief that it will be improving for their children—or, at least, less harmful than Internet porn or those computer games with titles like Garth, Gonad Crusher, meets the Predator Slimeball from Hell.

They are mistaken. Infotainment talks down to its public; it offers neither educational value nor satisfying entertainment. Because it dissembles, it is Bullshit.

"Infomercial," however, is merely an oxymoron. However you dress it up, it's an ad.

inspirational speaker (n.) Huge hair, dazzling teeth, hot-chocolate voice. The message is always the same: you can do anything if you set your mind to it. Look at me—I sailed in a bathtub across the Arctic Ocean wearing only my cut-off jean shorts before building myself this lucrative career on the lecture circuit.

instant classic (marketing hype) An oxymoron.

intimate (adj.) This has several meanings. Sentimental (of some nauseating gift), atmospheric (scented candles), sexy (perfume laden with some animal product like musk or civet), or tiny (of apartments). None of these usages is completely honest.

junk mail (np.) These are serious Bullshit. They have become horribly sophisticated. Here is just a selection of their techniques:

- Make the contents varied. Lots of different bits of multicolored paper excite the curiosity. Seal some in internal envelopes.
- Create the appearance of good luck so the recipient feels that he or she is already ahead of the game. Some element that looks like a gamble or a lottery is seductive. What the recipient does not know is

that every scratch card or perforated envelope in the entire mailing is a winner.

- Insert the recipient's name and address a lot so that the offer seems personal. Laser printing and mail merge software make this easy. The marketing psychologists (intellectual prostitutes or what?) tell us that we feel rewarded by seeing our names. Hence the copy that says, "Wouldn't you, *Mr. Webb*, be thrilled to be the only person in *Whatsit Road* to possess a brand new…"
- Use color printing that allows the signature on the letter to appear to be cursive and inky, as if the sales director/CEO signed your particular letter (along with all five million copies of the mailing). Most of us are not fooled by this, but it is mischievous.
- Get the recipient's adrenaline racing and heart surging with greed by enclosing what for just a moment looks like a real check. Of course, it's merely a sample of what we might win if only we enter the competition and buy a year's subscription to *Sad Bastard Weekly*.
- Tease out the process with a preliminary mailing that uses an exciting envelope offering prizes. More is coming! Watch out for it! "You, *Mr. Webb*, have already been selected—and you're the only one on your street!" Poor mailman, piledriven into the ground by the weight of this crap, will give the lie to that.
- Promise everybody a prize. It might only be a cardboard photo frame, but we all want something for nothing. Remember that by responding—even if we do not buy the product—we are giving some creepy marketing company information that they can use against us or sell.
- As long as the schmuck commits, offer a free trial. Don't make it too obvious that this is contingent on signing a direct debit instruction. The marketing people know that sheer inertia and the bore of doing the admin make it unlikely that we will cancel it after the free period has elapsed.

- Employ the best copywriters in the business. They will massage, cajole, persuade, and appeal to our basest instincts with copy so sparkling that in other circumstances, the writers could have been poets.

It would take a book to analyze all the sneaky marketing techniques in mail shots.

just released (adj. phrase) See **new**.

lifestyle (n.) A decision to buy one thing rather than another is now a lifestyle choice, an existential upheaval reflecting everything about the unspeakably super person that is you. One recent ad shows a freezing cool, preposterously good-looking male model all in black on a giant leather chair. He gazes solemnly to camera while the copy asserts that a wristwatch says more about you than anything else ever can. We do not have lives anymore. We have lifestyles. See also **style**.

limited edition (np.) The first production run of anything will be limited— how could it not be unless the manufacturer makes an infinite number? This is an appeal to exclusivity. In fact the limitation is only a matter of how many can be sold. You can be sure that if the item goes well there will be another limited edition "by popular demand."

loyalty card (np.) If you spend a fortune with one chain and possess one of their loyalty cards, eventually you will get enough points to buy, oh I don't know, a free chocolate bar and a copy of the *National Enquirer*. In the meantime the chain will have a detailed profile of you. Your taste in DVDs, your appetite for chicken korma? The six bottles of Burgundy and the economysized packet of condoms you bought in anticipation of a naughty weekend? Equipped with this knowledge, the chain will be able to target you with pro- motions that key in to your appetites. "Loyalty" is a clever word for such icy mercantile cleverness. In some stores these cards are called "privilege" cards—another word with a manipulative subtext.

luxury (n. and adj.)

> *Let not the royal bed of Denmark be*
> *A couch for luxury and damned incest*
> —William Shakespeare, Hamlet

Luxury has always had a connection with sex as well as opulence. The copywriters draw from this well of sensuality when they use the word. Socks, chocolate bars, wallpaper, cars, hotels, seats on airplanes—all these experiences are surreptitiously offering you physical pleasure.

massive, mega, mighty (adj.) We do like alliteration.

new (adj.) The most enduring of all the advertising words, "new" (like "latest") is an important claim for those people for whom it is a facet of status. It's bound to induce neurosis given that the process of becoming not new starts immediately.

offer ends... (promotional claim) A ploy as old and corny as "Hurry while stocks last..."

performance (n.) We live in an era obsessed with performance. Manufacturers understand this and make a range of "performance clothing." It's dressing up for adults. Velcro fastenings, hidden hoods, breathable fabrics, innumerable pockets (some hidden), day-glo colors visible by rescue helicopter pilots, wicking inner linings, storm cuffs, and waterproof zips—all this stuff is the sartorial equivalent of the gentle urbanite's purchase of a four-wheel drive car. Both are marketed the same way: find the explorer in you, overcome your limits... They are props for our fantasy lives.

prestige (n.) You're the kind of person who has bought one of our thingies. Respect! Respect! Also real-estate speak for a development, probably on a flood plain, of huge, ugly, cheaply-built houses complete with a double garage and a breathtaking price tag.

Price breakthrough! (n.) It's cheap, but without the connotations of that word.

prizes (n.) Fantastic prizes with a value "up to" $40,000! There's just one of those, a car chiseled at a hefty discount out of the garage that supplies the dealership's other vehicles. (The dealer has an inventory problem and can account for this near giveaway under his marketing budget.) The rest of the prizes—all quoted at maximum face value—could be useful packets of doilies or shiny pen sets.

Holiday prizes are particularly popular as promotional giveaways because travel companies will unload surplus capacity for almost nothing. It's better for a package-tour operator to fill the hotel with people spending money than leave it half empty—even if the airlines have to fly them to their destination for the airport tax plus a dollar.

When the promotion yells "prizes worth millions of dollars," note the lack of an indefinite article. It's not "a prize worth millions." Aggregating all the prizes at maximum value might—with some optimistic rounding—amount to a million (though who's checking?). The world of merchandising promotions runs on contacts, deals, and favors (all meticulously calibrated). No insider pays full price for anything.

product placement (np.) A whole new source of income for really crappy movies. The most egregious example is 1997's *The Saint* with Val Kilmer. The camera lingered on every brand name. At one point Kilmer awkwardly lifts up his laptop for no reason other than to show its logo to the camera. How much was negotiated for that movement? Ian Fleming may have started the whole fetishistic brand-name snobbery when he gave James Bond his first Rolex back in the 1950s.

Product placement dishonestly hides its commercial messages in the fabric of some other narrative, and that makes it Bullshit.

rare opportunity (marketing lie) That is, until the next one...

reassuringly expensive (adj. phrase) This expression is the "shout line" for a brand of so-so fizzy lager notable for the cost and inventiveness of its TV and cinema adverts. With disarming transparency, the copy relies on the notion that expensive equals good, a notion that is deeply ingrained in us despite often being wrong. No such equation holds in an age of value-added branding. Expensive equals expensive.

retail therapy (np.) This expression spread like flu. Where did it come from? Probably New York in the 1980s. Is there anything so decadent? Life is empty, so fill it with purchases. Marketing people have stripped the expression of irony.

sex (n.) Sells everything from photocopiers to insurance. We live in a commercial world of constant low-level titillation.
    If you're not getting enough—Buy more stuff!

statement (n.) This innocuous word has recently been kidnapped by the pretentious. Everything can make a statement now. A handbag, for instance, or a haircut. Something similar has happened to "signature." Star chefs in restaurants where even the starters are a week's wages have been known to utter expressions like "my signature crème brûlée" without laughing.

style (n.) When the historians of the future (if there is one) come to write about our times, the word that will most neatly encapsulate our narcissistic, masturbatory self-regard is "style." What is it? You are supposed to recognize it when you see it. Endless magazines and innumerable supplements in the papers write about it. The latest gadget, the latest hairstyle, the smartest kitchen, the right laces to wear in the right sneakers—all these are manifestations of that most desirable quality, style. Fashion used to move like the planet on an annual course, but now—and not entirely in jest—style victims will talk about something as "so last week." Style is said to be a personal expression, so it is paradoxical that the word is so often used by the marketing people of global brands.

Thus march we playing to our final rest. Fighting for breath, gasping for the last drop of clean water—but looking great.

supermarket layout (n.) The cleverest minds fine tune the geography of supermarkets with the aim of getting us to buy more.

Adult eye level is the most valuable real estate in the shop, so it is used for a cunning mix of basics and naughty value-added (i.e., expensive) luxuries. A subtlety is that the latter will be positioned to the right of the staples so that right-handed shoppers will find it easy to pick them up. Bulky "must-have" goods—industrial bales of diapers, for example—can be at ground level in the least attractive corner because we will ransack the store to find them. Milk will usually be on the back wall to ensure that there is something to draw us right into the depths of the building.

The items in a "sensible" shopping basket are distributed all over the place so that we shoppers must weave up and down the aisles (often retracing our footsteps) for miles while being exposed to the maximum amount of other goodies. This will also carry us past the largest number of aisle ends where promotional items or those soon to pass their expiration date are positioned. Occasionally there will be clusters of items that go together, but only if research shows that is rewarding. (Tea bags next to the expensive biscuits, champagne with the roses?) The whole environment will be temperature-controlled and drenched with ambient lift music, the rhythm keyed to our heartbeats. Delicious and comforting bread-making smells will be wafted through the air conditioning. Snares for the unwary—chocolate chip cookies, magazines full of yet more stuff to covet—lie in wait for us at the checkout.

Hidden cameras monitor the traffic flow and the analysts constantly tweak the design. Every week the managers share intelligence about what has worked well in individual stores so that the whole network can try it. Just in case regular shoppers get to know the layout, they change it anyway.

Really, what chance have we got? Unless we have the discipline of a Marine Corps drill sergeant, we are soon in a trance, empty-eyed, drifting up and down those aisles filling a vast trolley with stuff we never knew we needed. How many of us come out with only the items we went in for?

SUV (n.) Once upon a time, America was a frontier country. A man—a leathery, no-nonsense sort of man—could go squinty-eyed from looking into the sun at uncountable numbers of charismatic megafauna as they thundered in clouds of dust, flies, and poo across the rolling hills. This man's only vehicle, a sturdy Palomino; on his saddle, a Remington. Nature, apparently infinite, was there to be tamed. Life was dangerous.

Now that man works in an office. He's an account executive in a brand management company; he lives in the suburbs with his second wife, Marcella, an attorney specializing in intellectual property. They have one child, Nathan, a ten-year-old with a precocious talent for computer games.

Marcella drives a top-of-the-range Honda likely to run until the end of time or until the gas gives out—whichever is sooner. But he drives a huge quasi-military SUV the size of a cathedral. It boasts four-wheel drive, a colossal iron V-8 engine, and tires that would not look out of place on a truck.

What is going on here? Forget the rationalizations about this great big vehicle being safer. It is not. Although it is true that kinetic energy is $1/2 mv^2$—and there is a lot more "m" (mass) in a big vehicle than in a car—SUVs have a poor crash record, partly because their center of gravity is high and partly because of the over-confidence they induce in their drivers. What's more, modern small vehicles are constructed with rigid passenger cages and energy-absorbing crumple zones, refinements that the manufacturers of behemoths regard as unnecessary.

No. The man may work like a dog at the office, yet somehow he feels that life is too easy. He can put his vast vehicle into Drive and cruise down to a supermarket where he and Marcella can buy everything they need a hundred pounds at a time—and all packaged so hygienically that you cannot imagine the meat ever ran about a field. Instead of this being a source of joy, it is vaguely unsatisfying. Shouldn't he have a rack on the back window with a rifle loaded for bear?

All this applies even more to pick-up trucks. The Ford F150, and its gigantic phallic brethren, are among America's bestselling vehicles—and they are not just bought by construction workers who need haulage capacity. Gentle accountants, two days drive from the nearest wilderness, clamber into the cabs of these monsters, thrill to the bass rumble of the enormous engines, and soon drift off into a fugue state in which their mettle is put to the test somewhere out there in the distant mountains rather than the New Jersey turnpike.

A deep, atavistic appetite is at work. It's related to the one that makes the NRA such a powerful lobby and chunky Timberland boots and check shirts from L.L. Bean so appealing.

Just manufacturing these silly machines, yet alone fuelling them, is a catastrophe requiring the importation of vast quantities of oil. In terms of its foreign policy and trading deficit, America pays a terrible price for its addiction to energy—to say nothing of the damage to our one and only planet.

Come on, guys, enough is enough.

tasteful (adj.) Shouldn't we be the judge of that? The copywriter is reassuring people who are uncertain in practice about what it means. "Tasteful" is applied preferentially to wood or stainless steel.

technology (n.) Computer technology—okay. But shampoo technology? Pencil technology? Jackets made of breathable fabrics are now described as incorporating the latest in materials technology.

telephone marketing (np.) Imagine a monster-sized space lit by the regulation number of recessed fluorescent tubes (category three lighting) complete with dead flies. It's somewhere grim where the rent is low and the labor cheap. Dozens of women and a few odd men are sitting wearing headsets in front of computer screens in ranks of work-station hutches. They have been given a script and are under pressure to make so many calls per hour (something that is automatically monitored); they never know when their supervisor is listening in to them. Nearly all the people they call do not want to hear from them.

Their company has bought some database with your number in it—not the phone book, but something much more sophisticated. The company thinks it knows something about you already from your zip code and credit record. It might even have a detailed picture of your spending from your loyalty cards or be aware that you bought a security system in 1987. The women in this room are not paid much, but they win a bonus for every likely prospect whose details they can get into the computer. It's the mercantile equivalent of telephone sex—pitiable, desperate, slightly more hygienic than the real thing. No matter how irritated you are by the call, try to be kind.

terms and conditions apply (caveat in microscopic type) We should read them. Some of them are the nearest thing to penal servitude since the British navy press-ganged drunks into taking the King's Shilling and sent them off to sea.

traditional (adj.) Along with "heritage," this hurrah word evokes all the solid certainties of the past along with the comforting sense that anything traditional has long since won the good taste seal of approval—despite the fact that much of it was designed last week. Sometimes, in contrast to "modern," it means made of wood or covered with a wood veneer (often referred to as a real wood veneer).

Prepared meals made with traditional recipes are illustrated with a matronly figure with a kind face stirring a kettle on a farmyard. The actual factory, in industrial New Jersey, makes thousands of pounds at a time.

up to (prep.) See **prizes**.

warehouse sale (np.) A large shed miles from anywhere with no staff. Popular with computer geeks who either don't notice the horrible environment or believe it confers a kind of gritty romance. Usually cheaper than the high street, warehouses are strictly for buffs who read technical manuals for pleasure.

[a] whole new concept in... (hype) washing machines, paper clips, socks... In fact it's the same old stuff repackaged.

PART FIVE

Professional Bullshit:
Guarding the Mysteries

The man who reads nothing at all is better educated than the man who reads nothing but newspapers.

—Thomas Jefferson

Professionals are eager to assert their status. Before they qualify, doctors spend years being woken up in the night, half mad with fatigue, to stitch up fractured bodies or peer down some ravaged orifice. They do not take kindly to some layperson claiming their expertise, for it was hard won, or pretending to have it by stealing their technical language. In fairness to them, the body and its ailments are so fantastically complex that an agreed lexicon of terms is essential.

Lawyers are on shakier ground. They do enjoy some marvelous Latin tags and obscure terms like "tort" and "estoppel," but much of their everyday discourse is readily intelligible by a non-lawyer. The kindest view of legal jargon is that it facilitates communication between lawyers. A cynic might suggest that it is as well to keep everything as arcane as possible if you are charging hundreds of dollars per hour.

Accountants, architects, real estate agents, social workers, IT managers, journalists, and a host of other trades and professions have specialized vocabularies of their own. Most of these words and phrases are technical, an aid to economical information exchange, but some are designed (or at least used) as camouflage that hides its nature from the public gaze, but remains perfectly transparent to those in the know. Here are just a few examples.

---

addiction (medical/social services) Some substances such as alcohol, nicotine, and opiates affect the brain chemistry of constant users to the extent that ceasing consumption is difficult or even agonizingly painful. In addition to the metabolic changes in their bodies, a host of psychological factors and other life problems exacerbate the difficulty of escape from dependency for sufferers. Such addicts need all the help we can provide for their own sake and that of society at large.

However, we like to medicalize the human condition. We have therapy for grief (and tranquilizers to take the edge off it). Counseling is prescribed for bad behavior or unhappy relationships. Michael Douglas famously suffered from an addiction to sex, a tragic *medical* condition clearly nothing to do with him being fecklessly promiscuous. In keeping with this general reluctance to appear moralizing, drug dependency units are known as substance abuse treatment centers.

By labeling such appetites as addictions, we cease to be truly responsible for our own actions and become victims of circumstance—like someone catching flu. Some people describe themselves, unsmilingly, as addicted to shopping or web surfing. Marion Barry, the delinquent mayor of Washington, D.C. who was caught by the FBI on camera buying cocaine, excused his behavior with the line: "It was the drugs talking." The voters must have sympathized—or not cared either way—for he was eventually re-elected.

There's something else at work also. The media love addiction. In an orgasm of prurience, journalists report it in a manner that wobbles uneasily between condemnation and celebration. Addiction has all the perverse romance of bad behavior; it's the beautiful and the damned drinking and doping to death. A supermodel's boyfriend photographed gray and shaking in the back of a police van confers a kind of celebrity. Addiction sounds edgy. The sufferer appears so haunted and gloomy—quite interesting, in other words, especially if the alternative is looking like a self-indulgent, dim slob.

assets disproportionate to his income (journalistic code) Quarried from the excellent English language newspapers in India, this expression—softened for legal reasons with some locution like "X appears to have…"—means only one thing: corruption.

care in the community (social work catchphrase) Means kicking disturbed people out of hospital. You cannot find a social worker who will utter these words without a sigh.

Back in the 1950s and 60s, two new generations of drugs were developed (tricyclics and monoamine oxidase inhibitors) that promised effective treatment of depression without the side effects of earlier treatments. This, plus constant budgetary pressure and the feeling that big asylums were an unfashionable leftover from Victorian times, led to the closing of many bespoke mental institutions. Patients would instead be cared for in the community.

The trouble was that many patients did not return to stable homes in which loving relatives would ensure they took their medication, and social workers, of whom there is a finite supply, could not be there all the time. Many patients were discharged into distinctly terrible circumstances and soon found themselves on the street, often to be seen—to the dismay of passersby—having intense conversations with people not actually present. The trend continued into the 1990s when another new class of drugs, the selective serotonin re-uptake inhibitors (of which Prozac is the best known), came on the market.

There have been a handful of cases where unfortunates with dangerous mental illnesses like paranoid schizophrenia have been released into the community and, in the grip of some terrible delusion, have then murdered someone. See also **community** under Political Bullshit.

Chinese rejection (publisher's editorial device) Used for rejecting something too literary for the house. It goes something like this: though our publishing house may flourish for a thousand years and all our rivals crumble into the dust, yet we would still not be worthy...

commercial sex worker (np., social services) A prostitute.

consultative (educational adj.) See **participatory**.

CPD (acronym) Continuous Professional Development. If you're any good, you will try to keep up with news in your field. However, CPD looks impressive on your CV. Every few years, you go on a three-day course where you learn to speak of tipping points, make useful contacts, drink too much, and try to have an affair.

critically acclaimed (adj., publishing/arts) An okay review in the *Denver Post*.

cryptogenic (medical jargon) The doctor hasn't the faintest idea what you've got.

deaccession (museum curator's code) Putting the really boring stuff in the basement and letting it rot.

deconstruction (critical jargon) Nobody analyzes anymore. "Deconstruction" is analysis with a wicked French accent, dark glasses, and a cigarette holder. See **structuralism**.

disappointing (auditor's adj.) Urbane financial analysts' description of company results that have failed to reach target for the third successive quarter. Don't be fooled. Behind the scenes there's panic dumping of stock or an icy assessment of takeover prospects.

easy access to... (real estate code) Yes, you can walk.

empowerment (social services/political) A relentlessly overused hurrah word. Despite being on the lips of legions of well-intentioned people for a good decade, the old power structures are still in place.

encapsulation (journalistic technique) It's not the word here that is bullshit, but the process—and perhaps it should not be made to bear too much weight as it's difficult to see how else to sidle up to a story. The bullshit factor may rest as much with the reader as the perpetrator.

Journalists are universally trained to "encapsulate" a story, to open it with a paragraph that gives the big picture, while subsequent copy provides progressively more detail. It's called the inverted pyramid structure and it's designed to let the reader scan and then decide whether or not to read on in the confidence that he or she already has the gist. Rendering down something complex to a salty first paragraph takes practice and may do the report a subtle mischief. Sometimes the nuances are all. Occasionally, if you can be bothered to read all the story, you find yourself not agreeing with the synoptic opening. People who only ever read the first paragraph skate over the world of information and end up with no real understanding how any of it pertains to anything. If you can be bothered to "turn to page 17" when instructed at the bottom of a column you will appear to be paranormally well-informed.

environment (n.) This important word is often a grace note in professional advertisements. Teachers no longer work in school; they work in a school environment. Business people operate in an office environment.

experiences (n.) We don't visit a hospital—we have a hospital experience. A well-known travel company specializing in adventure (i.e., uncomfortable) holidays offers "real life experiences." Are we somehow putting a frame around everything we do as if it were just another episode in the novel or movie in which we star? With MP3 players, we can now customize a soundtrack for our lives.

five minutes' walk from... (real estate code) An Olympic athlete in training might do it in five.

further and better particulars (legal code) An adjournment is often sought in court so that these can be disclosed. Quite often it means that the lawyer has not read the case notes yet or the office has lost them.

grant (n.) There is just too much scientific language for inclusion in *The Dictionary of Bullshit* and much of it is a perfectly legitimate aid to comprehension between peers. Science is an attempt to find out how the universe works. It pushes back the horizon of human knowledge using a method designed to ensure that every inch gained is defensible. Science is the greatest achievement of the human spirit.

Unfortunately that does not stop some of it from being trivial, self-serving, in thrall to commercial or military funding, and (very rarely) fraudulent. While many PhDs are badly paid, equipment is expensive and big science, like high-energy physics, needs the kind of money that only national or international budgets can provide.

It takes an exceptionally honest sponsor to pay for research that produces a result that is damaging to the sponsor's interests. The most important word in the entire lexicon of modern science is "grant." The research may be meticulous, in which case we need not ask who paid— and who benefits—from the findings. Not all academics and researchers, however, are dispassionate seekers after truth.

I am instructed… (legal cliché) Even the wicked and the inarticulate (especially the latter) are entitled to representation. In the American legal system, a lawyer should not knowingly lie in court. He or she must tell the truth as it has been conveyed by the defendant. Whatever doubts lawyers may have in the privacy of their minds, they must present the client in the best possible light. However, there are occasions when they are obliged to tell a story so ludicrous that it is difficult to do so without their eyes bulging with insincerity. In those circumstances, they utter the words "I am instructed…" with a special emphasis, as if talking in italics. Here's an example in which nearly everyone, except the person in the dock, understands the code:

"*I am instructed*, Your Honor, that my client, Gnasher Williams, was driving along—innocently going about his business at 3 a.m.—when he spotted a safe full of money on the pavement. Some poor soul must have lost that, he thought to himself, so as a responsible citizen I'd better just pop it in the trunk of the car and take it to the nearest police station. It was at this moment that the arrival of the squad car saved him the trouble..."

icon/iconic (critical/pop culture) Once icons were religious images from the Greek or Russian Orthodox Church. They are exquisitely made, often with lots of gold leaf, but they lack perspective and can get a bit repetitive. Then there were computer icons. Now any object or image that some journalist or commentator reckons is characteristic of its time, or just ubiquitous, is "iconic." Che, T-shirts, Beatle haircuts, Sony Walkmans—all are icons. The word is devalued to the point where it should only be used with imaginary quotation marks.

idiopathic (medical jargon) God knows what this ailment is. The doctor doesn't, but has a vague intuition that it has arisen spontaneously from within the patient rather than an external source.

liability (legal concept) Liability is a responsibility for some obligation, especially that of assuming a debt or other financial burden such as compensation. It has become a magic word that, once uttered, produces all kinds of odd behavior. Enough has been written about the American appetite for litigation and there are even websites devoted to keeping aficionados up to speed with the latest absurdities.

The liability culture has begun to cover the globe. Manufacturers cover their products with warnings, no matter how unnecessary they may appear. DO NOT USE THIS PESTICIDE AS A COFFEE SWEETENER! You will have seen this kind of thing and wondered why. It's a matter of product liability. Local authorities try to avoid liability by instructing social workers to do everything "by the book," no matter how inappropriate the book may be in individual cases.

Doctors may order procedures and tests that are time-consuming, expensive, or even painful to avoid the risk of liability in the event of a mishap. "So," the anxious doctor imagines some lawyer saying in an expensive and career-threatening action, "you did not feel it necessary *in your experience* [sneering tone at this point] to give my tragic client an MRI scan for her sprained wrist…" Better to be safe and do everything.

There's little to be done about the fear of liability. Blaming someone is a deep human need. We are stuck with it. For your amusement, try tossing the word like a hand grenade into correspondence with local government.

Kafkaesque (criticism/arts) Bleak, probably unintelligible, best avoided… Even more commercially damaging than "sensitive."

light year (multiple misuses) A mind-bendingly large unit of distance $(9.46 \times 10^{12}$ kilometers)—*not* a unit of time. A light year is so impossibly huge that it is only of practical use to astronomers—and they, for technical reasons, prefer another unit, the parsec (3.26 light years). Even more destructive to the imagination is the megaparsec. Light from the sun takes about eight minutes and twenty seconds to reach our planet.

matter of principle (np.) In legal circles, it is understood that you have to pay for your principles. A principle is a universal moral imperative, but it is confused surprisingly often with a blow to some chap's distended ego. If both sides believe something is a matter of principle they will keep plugging away at it long after anybody sensible would have settled. Good lawyers will sigh when they hear the expression. Bad ones will calculate their fees.

[in] need of modernization (real estate code) It's a wreck.

negative care outcome (medical/social services jargon) Death. Bizarrely, this is not a parody. It was first spotted in the 1980s and has since spread.

negative coping mechanism (social services jargon) Usually prostitution.

non-specific (medical) As in "a non-specific viral infection." The doctor has not the foggiest notion of what you've got, but hopes this broad-spectrum antibiotic will knock it off. He or she knows you would feel shortchanged if it were just left to your immune system to do its work.

obituary code (journalists, for the use of) "Relentless raconteur" equals really boring. A "ladies' man" was an uncontrollable groper with satyriasis. "Confirmed bachelor" and "never married" used to be code for homosexual. "After a long illness" was once understood as a euphemism for cancer just as "after a brief illness" could mean suicide. "Larger than life" or "charismatic" could be code for a vain bully who never let anybody else talk. "Party girl" meant promiscuous. "Society model" was an up-market prostitute. In our less inhibited times such circumlocutions are no longer necessary.

original features (real estate code) It's a tip. There has been no modernization since the house was built in 1872.

participatory (educational adj.) Participatory decision-making means that the head teacher may tell the staff what's going to happen but not actually put it to the vote. The word sounds democratic, but isn't. **Consultative** democracy is similar.

[the] pencil (theatrical device) "We've got a pencil on Darren," the director might say to Darren's agent. Sometimes it's a light pencil, but it could be a heavy pencil. If the actor doesn't get the part, then "we're lifting the pencil." This is harmless bullshit designed to avoid lacerating feelings by baldly stating that the director has seen a carrot emote more convincingly than Darren. The pencil is also used by commissioning editors who might buy a project from an independent production company.

Another useful expression that disguises rejection with a pretended change of artistic policy is "we're going in another direction."

pencil in [a date] (v.) This means it is provisional until one or other party gets a better offer.

period features (real estate code) An old fireplace. "Many period features"—two fireplaces. The description may be as dangerous as **original features**.

post-modern irony (expression loved by critics) "Post-modern" has a clear meaning in the case of architecture. The modern movement or international style in the "built environment" was clean and functional with no dissembling about the mechanical demands of a building. Done well (and especially under a smiting light), it looked good. Indifferent execution, however, can be depressingly boring. Post-modern architecture is less austere and more frivolously inclined to decoration. The split pediment on the top of New York's AT&T skyscraper is a witty example.

But post-modern irony? Irony is irony. How has it changed? Critics tend to use this expression defensively about a recent film, book, piece of sculpture (indeed it seems applicable to anything) in which the artist, wearing a sly grin, makes a knowing or tongue-in-cheek reference. Douglas Adams remarked that he hated tongue-in-cheek because it means that you could not be bothered to do something properly. (See also "ironically" under **adverbs** in Political Bullshit.)

pull focus (social sciences/further education) Borrowed from filmmaking, this expression pretends that chairing a meeting is a techie mystery for men with designer haircuts and chunky divers' watches.

quantum leap (criticism/arts) A universally abused expression from physics that has come to mean grand, radical, and mold breaking. The Pauli Exclusion Principle states that no two elementary particles like electrons can have the same quantum numbers as they move between different energy states. The leap or jump between these states is a discontinuous process—but unimaginably tiny.

season (arts admin/TV schedule code) If you can connect some items, no matter how negligible the link, pretend you've got a plan by calling the result a "season." Three horrid movies featuring Kurt Russell, for instance, definitely constitute a season.

self-deliverance (medical/social services) Suicide.

situation (n.) This usually innocent though overused word exemplifies Bullshit when it is employed as a means of sneaking away from personal responsibility. A situation is, after all, a prevailing state of affairs, a confluence of circumstance—a given. If some clammy man in a suit says, "Gee, I'm sorry, but we're not in a payment situation," it's not the result of individual will. Nobody wanted this to happen or, God forbid, mismanaged the accounts, transferred the funds to the Cayman Islands, or simply ran out of money. Of course, it's a situation—something built into the nature of the universe.

Sometimes, "situation" may be tact. Why lacerate feelings if you can blame something unpleasant on abstraction? (The firm is in a non-promotion situation.) But frequently, the word indicates moral cowardice, a pretense that something is not only beyond your gift but that it had nothing to do with any of your decisions in the first place. A pension fund shortfall situation, for instance.

The word's appearance in such fraught circumstances has lent it a secondary meaning peculiar to American English—namely, that something has gone wrong. These days, astronaut James Lovell, the commander of the Apollo 13 mission, would not have uttered the famous words: "Houston, we have a problem." "Houston, we have a situation…" would be understood by all.

soft landing (economic slang) Gentle recovery from some economic blow or incipient recession (in contrast to a hard landing). The metaphor is vivid. It's only bullshitty to the extent that such slang exists to convince outsiders that there are mysteries not easily fingered by the uninitiated. The expression "dead cat bounce" is also worthy on grounds of graphic power. A dead cat may rebound when dropped from a city tower, but it's still dead. Analogously, a market may stage a small rally after a catastrophic fall.

structuralism (criticism/arts) Structuralism turns on the idea that any element in a system of communication can only be understood in relation to other components in the system and that all such systems have fundamental features in common—e.g., they encode, decode, and transmit information. The practical result of this is that the critic can gain useful insights by looking at the distribution and frequency of the signs and symbols in the system (by counting key words, for instance) and that those insights will be free from the ideological baggage that comes with taking into account any background knowledge of the author and his or her culture. Ferdinand de Saussure, Roland Barthes, and Claude Lévi-Strauss (who applied the approach to anthropology) are the essential names to drop.

This is not entirely Bullshit, though it has had a dismal effect on the intelligibility of those in the English-speaking world who follow its precepts. It is rather like French lingerie—naughty, intriguingly European, and not very comfortable. The following bit of doggerel is helpful:

This is the creed'a
Jacques Derrida.
There ain't no author.
There ain't no reader, eeda.

studio (real estate code) A studio apartment is a tiny one-room hovel a few inches larger than "a closet" and just a bit smaller than "intimate."

the successful candidate... (advertising) There is a curious standard diction in job advertisements, especially those placed by headhunters, employment agencies, or local government. Interpersonal and communication skills, the ability to motivate a team, a clear vision, a proven track record, personal commitment in a challenging environment, passion, a familiarity with quality audit processes, a vibrant personality, goal-oriented management processing, and a talent for saying "proactive" without snickering (no, the last is made up)—all these virtues will qualify you for an astonishing range of jobs from equal-opportunity employers offering "rewarding packages." Only the reference to the track record suggests you need know anything much about the job itself.

[a] surprising change of form (journalistic code in horse racing) A superior horse has been taken out for a gallop five times with instructions to the jockey not to win. The animal's form now makes it look like a tin of dog food on the hoof. Then before its sixth outing it is heavily fancied off-track with the bookmakers. The horse romps home at about Mach One, leaving the other nags in its wake and cleaning up satisfactorily for those in the know. The journalists understand what has happened, but obviously cannot say so. Hence the code.

syndrome (medical) Once this was a medical term for a set of signs and symptoms that, taken together, form a recognizable condition. Gulf War Syndrome, for example, manifests itself in many unpleasant ways; its existence was denied for years until research showed that multiple vaccinations and massive doses of anti-nerve gas agents like pyridostigmine bromide were a damaging insult to a soldier's body. Some syndromes have a grim hilarity. "Sedentary Death Syndrome" has recently entered pathologists' language to describe enormously fat people, gorged on junk food, flat-lining in front of the TV.

Recently the word, with all its quasi-medical authority, has spread to cover many kinds of psychological complexities and clusters of symptoms. Chinese Restaurant Syndrome, for example, was widely thought to be induced by the frequent enjoyment of Chinese food because of the wide use in restaurants of monosodium glutamate (MSG) as a flavor enhancer. The condition is entirely fictitious.

Linguists have a smart word for the process whereby naming an abstraction appears to summon it into being: "reification." Except for works of fiction, we expect names to refer to concepts and objects in the world. We observed things and gave them labels. We should be cautious about doing it the other way around—naming something and then finding it.

threshold (n.) This word is often borrowed from the physical sciences. In biology, for example, it means the minimum stimulus that will produce a response in irritable tissue. The popular context in which the word is often found is safety. A safety threshold for some environmental pollutant is the level below which no harmful effects have been detected. That is not the same as saying that the pollutant is safe at that level; it might be, but it is also possible that the effects are too slow or subtle to be detectable given the current state of the art.

After the Chernobyl disaster in April 1986, there was a huge increase in thyroid cancers in youngsters in Belarus, the Ukraine, and Russia. This was surprising, as the radiation from iodine-131 released by the accident was too low—according to the threshold model—to have caused the increase. However, the thyroid glands of children are especially sensitive to radiation.

Threshold studies are complex and often need decades to produce results. Even then they can be equivocal, as it is difficult to isolate the effect of one environmental insult when we are awash in a bath of chemicals, food additives, and atmospheric fall-out interacting in ways we do not fully understand. Some substances have an affinity for the fatty tissues of the body but others, like the radio-iodine from Chernobyl, home in on organs where they can do more mischief.

The fact that the science is uncertain does not give us license to believe any old panicky nonsense put about by someone at least as uncertain, but it does mean that skepticism is in order.

UGC (broadcasting acronym) User-Generated Content. A term referring to vox pops and phone-ins. Most of us are not naturals with a microphone. The professional anchor men and women do their best to sound interested and not patronize us too badly, but these programs are generally dismal. However, they are cheap to make.

UPD (medical and social work acronym) Untreatable Personality Disorder. Someone with UPD is not mentally ill exactly, but just irredeemably horrible and difficult. Such judgments are inadmissible and have to be dressed up as a diagnosis.

Snappy acronyms are particularly useful for defending mysteries. Some professions, space engineers for instance, have almost lost the power of everyday speech.

up and coming (real estate code) The area is grim. Spend the money you save on a flack-jacket.

What have you done? (IT manager's cry) You haven't done anything, and you mustn't let some techie make you feel guilty. The stupid machines with their fearsome error messages (SHUT DOWN IMMEDIATELY. THIS PROGRAM HAS PERFORMED AN ILLEGAL OPERATION.) should damn well do what you want. Most of the time they stop because they are whimsically contrary, and the software is far too complicated.

With respect... (adv. phrase) In legal circles, this is code for "you are a nincompoop." The greater the respect, the greater the degree of contempt. "With the greatest respect..." is almost actionable.

without prejudice (essential legal expression) Imagine you are a publisher locked into a legal action against someone who claims to have been libeled. You've got your lawyers, he's got his, and both of you have backed off snarling and growling into your respective corners. Regardless of the rights and wrongs of the matter, you are losing sleep over the sheer cost of defending the case. Every time you say "Good morning" to your lawyer it seems to cost $400. Your opponent knows this, and he's suffering too. Both of you talk a strong game and maintain that you are determined to pursue the issue relentlessly through the courts until the very end of time. You're damned if you will compromise. Besides, in the dance of advance and retreat that you are both performing with such disregard to your overdrafts, showing weakness would be a tactical error.

128

Long before any action gets to court, a great deal of expensive correspondence will have been exchanged between the lawyers. A "without prejudice" letter—or it could be a conversation—is a means of having a practical negotiation. Except in special circumstances, nothing declared "without prejudice" can be produced in court.

So what happens? Your lawyer's open letter (on the record and available as evidence) says that the complaint has no merit. The text in question is not defamatory, the opponent is not identified nor is he identifiable and, besides, that bit about sex in wet suits full of warm marmalade happens to be true. The author has affidavits to that effect witnessed by the Archbishop of Canterbury. In short, the plaintiff's action is an entirely mischievous put-on. What's more, the lawyer's client's quality of life has already been adversely affected; he will countersue for exemplary damages citing loss of profit, interference with his business, mental distress, and the full recovery of his costs. The failure of the other side to keel over promptly will result in further grimly expensive and punitive action. The sky will fall.

Meanwhile, accompanying this blast, the "without prejudice" letter, which for obvious reasons should not repeat any of the accusations, asks whether the other side will accept five hundred bucks to go away.

"Without prejudice" is a pragmatic device that lawyers use all the time. It is useful, but also a piercing reminder that the civil law is a game not overly concerned with the truth. Sometimes the outcome of the game fortuitously coincides with some notion of justice. Lawyers have had centuries to adjust the rules of the game so that only they can play, and in many actions it is the cost of the players rather than the rightness of the cause that drives those caught up in the game to settle.

you must be so tired (theatrical gush) Actors have a range of over-the-top euphemisms. Imagine you're a thespian invited backstage by a friend who has just put in a performance as wooden as a tree stump. Frankly it stank, but what can you say? Theatrical egos are vast but vulnerable. Hence: "*Darling*, you must be so tired!" Forehead-slapping amazement, which could be interpreted as admiration by someone primed to do so, can also do the trick: "Gosh, you've done it again!"

There is a well-known director whose tact in rehearsal has resulted in the catchphrase: "Wonderful! Let's do it again."

PART SIX

New Age and Alternative Bullshit:
Finding Your Inner Child

The most incomprehensible thing about the world is that it is comprehensible.

—Albert Einstein

The fact that we exist at all is astonishing. We're bits of stuff driven by the same push/pull material causality that works the inanimate universe, yet we are configured with such complexity that we can think. What's more, we have compelling theoretical reasons for believing that some of our thoughts are relevant to the entire cosmos. This improbable predicament of matter has come about through the working of the powerful tautology of evolution—what survives, survives. And all this has happened on a tiny speck of rock revolving around an ordinary star in what Douglas Adams called the unfashionable end of the Milky Way, a colossal galaxy that is just one of billions.

The current state of cosmology allows us to make elegant and testable predictions, but the model works by positing that what we can detect consists of only a fraction of what is out there. Science has by no means worked everything out, and probably never will. Yet the incompleteness of the picture does not give us the freedom to believe just anything. Scientific investigation can reveal what is there. Wishful thinking and credulity, on the other hand, can tell us what we would like to be there. A strong urge to believe a proposition does not make it the case. However hard you strain at imagining a million dollars in your bank account, you—and the bank—will expect more by way of evidence before you can spend it.

That's the problem of New Age thinking. It's thrilling; it titillates our sense of wonder without our having to work too hard at it. Science has opened a door on inexhaustible complexity and great beauty, but keeping the door open requires brain-cudgeling effort, close attention to detail, and endless checking of ideas by experiment and repetition. Such careful methods cannot hope to grip the imagination as immediately as dark forces, secret cabals, aliens with an appetite for experiments of odd sexual inventiveness on bored rural alcoholics, miracle cures, and all the other apparatus that is usually collected under the heading New Age or Forgotten Knowledge. It is such a pity, because under our noses there are mysteries more shocking than anything we can invent. A blade of grass, for example, is more complicated than a star.

If manifestations of New Age thinking were confined to airport best-sellers and internet conspiracy theories, perhaps the worst that could be said is that it is lazy and daft. Unfortunately things are darker than that. Insane cults have swept up the gullible and disturbed, usually leaving them more disturbed, broke, and, in extreme cases, dead. Mountains of fruitcake have been sculpted from genuinely interesting anomalies, and logic has died as believers construe positive and negative evidence in exactly the same way. (Please see the entry on **conspiracy** for an explanation of this claim.)

One particularly mischievous aspect of New Age thinking is "alternative" medicine, a vast and lucrative industry exploiting the credulous and the desperate. It is a shameful trade, and it is one that captures the central irony of the whole movement. New Age is all about self-improvement, or self-realization to give it a more alternative gloss. Either term contains the key word: "self." Whether it's for well-being, longevity, self-knowledge, or a tantric sex life, the New Ager is toiling away at individual benefit as selfishly as an ambitious corporate executive trying for promotion by reading an inspirational management guru.

The New Age puts humankind and their spirituality center stage. Isn't it time we grew up and tried, unflinchingly, to see our place in the universe without these invented comforts?

ad hoc (Latin term) Meaning "for the particular case," an ad hoc hypothesis is drafted in to an argument to meet a specific need. Such devices are often found in any discussion about New Age phenomena or the paranormal in general. The most common example is when some effect like telepathy or remote sensing cannot be replicated under stringent conditions. An ad hoc hypothesis comes to the rescue: such subtle effects are contingent on the positive states of mind of those present, so it is hardly surprising that they cannot be detected in the presence of skeptical investigators. The phenomenon is thus invulnerable to proper testing and becomes a matter of faith.

aliens (n.) The universe is big, so big in fact that really unlikely things can happen in it again and again. The odds against life evolving are very great, so it is just possible that our planet is supremely consequential. After all, life certainly happened here. Happily, the universe has room for an effectively infinite number of tries. Statistically, therefore, it is probable that life exists elsewhere in the universe. Unfortunately, the very thing that makes life so likely (the size of the universe) also massively reduces the likelihood of it wandering into our remote backwater at a time when we are around to observe it. Interested readers are referred to the famous Drake Equation that formalizes this calculation (see Appendix).

Despite the library of books on UFOs and their inhabitants, there is no reliable evidence that we have been visited. For some of us, especially in the remoter parts of the country, earthbound life seems prosaic so we are thrilled if the aliens turn up. Creatures with god-like powers from the sky are bound to produce a frisson with deep mythological antecedents.

The most commonly reported alien is the so-called "gray"—a small biped with huge, cruel, oval eyes, a tiny mouth, and a completely smooth body devoid of sexual characteristics. People who observe one of these have often read about them beforehand; they have the comfort of knowing that their alien will fit into an accepted taxonomy. The author Whitley Strieber wrote several bestsellers based on his unpleasant encounters with the grays. Many abductees report that the grays are particularly interested in fiddling with their victims' genital equipment.

Though there is a host of gorgeously elaborated conspiracy theories, there is no sign of aliens on Earth. Yet rumors—and books—persist. One of the most enduring stories is that an alien craft crashed near **Roswell**, New Mexico, in 1947. It has even been honored with its very own faked autopsy film. The more the authorities try to refute this story, the more convinced are the conspiracy theorists of its veracity. The powers-that-be would deny it, wouldn't they? Only the state has the resources to hide something so completely, after all. See **conspiracy** for further discussion of this logic.

alternative medicine (np.) This is in contrast with science-based western medicine, whose practitioners are seen as possessed by a mechanistic **paradigm** (see Corporate Bullshit). The body, according to this idea, is just a machine like a car. If you take it to the garage to have its fuel injection fixed, the specialist mechanic will not necessarily look at the rest of the vehicle. That's the position imputed to conventional doctors by believers in alternative medicine. "Conventional" in this context is pejorative—stodgy, closed to new ideas, accepting of received wisdom, and so on.

However, seeing the whole patient as a human being and not a self-propelled collection of symptoms has been orthodox teaching in medical schools for generations. Practitioners of conventional medicine are irritated at the suggestion that they are not as understanding and sensitive as alternative healers. Doubtless there are some cold clinicians, ever ready to prescribe potent pharmaceuticals wished upon them by sinister drug companies, but then there must be clod-hopping homeopaths and brutal reflexologists too. The crucial difference between conventional medicine and alternative therapies is that the latter are very unlikely to have been tested in any kind of controlled experiment. Instead they may rely on the power of suggestion (helpful only with psychosomatic ailments) or even be downright dangerous, either intrinsically or because they delay conventional treatment.

Alternative medicine also means non-western. The wisdom of the East has long been highly valued, and analysis confirms that many herbal remedies contain powerful chemical agents. However, in Ayurvedic and Chinese medicine there is much magical thinking whereby the characteristics of the unfortunate animal that provides the source of the treatment are believed to be transmitted to the patient. The stomach, with its seething mass of acid, bacterial flora, and enzymes, breaks down an extraordinary range of inputs from sources as disparate as steak tartar and tofu. A biochemical plant that could do the same is utterly beyond our current technological prowess, but our guts perform this wonder routinely. All is transformed into carbohydrates, minerals, protein, and all the other stuff the body needs, and the waste is eliminated. The basic components lose all trace of their origins.

For the sake of trade in Chinese medicine the world's most beautiful predator, the tiger, has been hunted almost to extinction. The northern white rhino is down to dozens of individuals. These unlikely two-ton creatures with their terrible eyesight and fantastic sense of smell are unlikely to survive because their horns make nifty dagger handles and, when powdered, are believed—mistakenly—to help aging oriental gentlemen with their droopy penises.

See also **complementary medicine** and **holistic**.

 angels (n.) These mostly benign creatures from Christian (and pre-Christian) mythology are messengers between man and God and can intercede for us if approached in the right spirit. Protestants were always a bit unsure about them, but Catholics rate angels highly. For many centuries they kept a low profile except as metaphors or in art, but in the 1980s and 90s they made something of a comeback, with many sightings by people who were ecstatic but not so awed that they could not recount their experiences on chat shows. Now you can find angels in paperback for only $6.95, or for a few hundred dollars a company in Texas will help you find one to suit your particular needs.

aromatherapy (n.) A tissue of nonsense complete with cute little bottles of essences and candle-powered china gizmos for evaporation. You can luxuriate in a warm bath scented with lovely perfumes or get a friend to massage your body with floral oils. It's sensual and relaxing. But then a chocolate éclair is also pleasurable and has much the same therapeutic value.

astrology (n.) An ancient symbol system based on the orbits of planets and the patterns (the signs of the zodiac) we have superimposed with a kind of join-the-dots creativity on the brighter stars visible by the human eye. Believers claim that the positions of the planets and stars at the time of birth or, according to Chinese astrology, at the time of conception furnish profound insight into character, and even offer predictive power. The symbols themselves are said to reflect fundamental human characteristics, though they are sufficiently ambiguous for an astrologer equipped with some pragmatic psychology and native intuition to read into them whatever seems appropriate.

It is difficult to overstate the extent to which astrology is nonsense.

After sex, millions of spermatozoa wiggle away on their grueling journey to fertilize an egg. Usually they all die in the attempt. If two succeed, the result is non-identical twins—two individuals who can be surprisingly different in character and outlook. If one fertilized egg splits, however, the result is monozygotic or identical twins, who have been demonstrated by studies of separation to show a degree of convergence that is disquieting for anyone with a liberal biology-is-not-destiny worldview. Nature and nurture, rather than the patterns in the sky, make us who we are.

But perhaps, an astrologer might say, the patterns exerted an influence on which sperm made it? Consider the scale. Suppose you shrunk the universe down by a factor of a million. The sun would be roughly a mile across, and the Earth would be forty-three feet in diameter and ninety-three miles from the sun. Shrink the universe again by another thousand times so it is now a billionth of its actual size. The sun is now just 4.3 feet across, the Earth about half an inch in diameter and only 490 feet from the churning nuclear fusion reactor that is the sun. Superimpose this image on somewhere you know, like your hometown. The sun could sit on home plate at Yankee Stadium and the Earth would be whizzing around like a demented marble at about the distance of a well-hit home run.

Where on the same scale would you find the nearest star? In a distant suburb? In the Midwest? In Mexico? In fact you would have to go a long way off the planet before our very nearest stellar neighbor came into view. Remember too that the patterns of the zodiac are artifacts in which some stars are thousands of light years further away than others to which they appear linked by the accident of perspective.

But no amount of reasoning will deter someone who wishes to believe. Consider the following dialogue, reproduced verbatim:

Skeptic: "How can such a brainy person as you believe this astrology baloney?"

Believer: "That is so like a Capricorn to be skeptical…"

Atlantis (proper n.) A fabled island, beautiful and prosperous, swallowed by the sea. It's made good copy ever since the time of Plato, who mentioned it in the *Timaeus*. Plato probably invented it for narrative effect, though scholars have suggested that some memory of a volcanic catastrophe may lie behind the story. Atlantis has been positively identified in dozens of locations and a library of books has been written on the subject. Being conveniently missing, the island tends to reflect the preoccupations of the authors at the time of writing. The Atlantis industry shows no sign of slowing down.

candling (n.) Take somebody ill, turn her on her side, and stick a candle in her ear. Light the candle and step well back as it magically sucks the poisons out of the body.

channeling (n.) Our bodies are but tawdry vehicles for a life force. We have lived many times before, invariably as *really interesting* people. Using the right hypnotic techniques, we can get in touch with our previous incarnations and channel them through our current form into the present. It shows how enormously creative and suggestible we can be in the right circumstances. See also **karma**.

complementary medicine (n.) Overlaps with **alternative medicine**, while sounding more benign as it explicitly acknowledges the role of orthodox medicine. However, it is a billion-dollar business run on ruthless capitalist lines.

conspiracy (n.) Conspiracies are much more exciting than the inadvertence and cock-up theories with which they are often contrasted. The World Wide Web is a place where conspiracy theories flourish. The authors of the many websites where these are expounded find it more frightening, by and large, to believe that there are people in control—no matter how venal and self-seeking they may be—than that the world bumbles along in an inchoate mess.

The best conspiracies start small and grow in a series of forehead-smiting revelations to embrace everything. An ideal conspiracy should uncover some odd anomaly and then creep outwards in tiny but arguable steps, using rhetorical questions of the "dare we not speculate..." and "surely we can see..." variety. Each new delicious revelation opens the way to include the Illuminati, the rustless pillar, the Cathars, Opus Dei, the Rosicrucians, the Bilderberg Group, Skull and Bones, the Freemasons and the Ordo Templi Orientis, and other arcana, some of it not confined to our planet.

From the Bullshit point of view this is elegant. Something so universal must have left evidence, and the very lack of it can only point to massive interventions. Only the very powerful could have covered something up so completely. Intellectually this reasoning is a little beauty that should command the kind of respect expressed by Yossarian, the anti-hero of Joseph Heller's classic, *Catch-22*:

> Yossarian was moved very deeply by the absolute simplicity of this clause of Catch-22, and let out a respectful whistle. "That's some catch, that Catch-22," he observed.
>
> "It's the best there is," Doc Daneeka agreed.

creationism (n.) Some Christians, especially members of evangelical churches, maintain that the biblical account of the making of the universe is literally true. The world is no older than the roughly six thousand years calculated by Bishop James Ussher in the seventeenth century from the generations listed in Genesis. The apparently great age of the Earth is an illusion: it was created that way, complete with the fossil record. This was the solution suggested in Victorian times by Philip Henry Gosse and still embraced in some quarters today. In Kentucky, there is a creationist museum that shows human beings and dinosaurs coexisting. The latter did not survive Noah's Flood.

Other creationists allow for a greater time scale but argue that the fossil record is incomplete. God, using the material already on hand, created man in one of the parts absent from the record—this giving rise to the theory known as "the God of the Gaps." Still others see the Genesis story as allegorical and the seven days of creation as corresponding to cosmological phases. In this version, "Let there be light" is identified with the Big Bang of cosmology. Recent controversy has focused on the "intelligent design" idea that maintains that biology in general and human beings in particular are too exquisitely complex and perfectly adapted to be the result of some random process like evolution. There must have been a supernatural artificer. For these Christians, "intelligent design" should be taught alongside evolution in schools.

There are too many varieties of creationism to be synopsized here, but what they all have in common is a belief in God and the rejection of evolution as the means by which we humans came to exist.

For creationists, evolution is "just a theory" and relegated to the status of the provisional. But a theory in science is not the same as the kind of theory one might advance in a bar about the fortunes of a football team. A scientific theory should be coherent, complete, and supported by observation. It has to be both explanatory and predictive.

Unlike creationism, evolution passes all these tests. It is the most powerful tautology we know—what survives, survives, and thus can reproduce. Evidence for it abounds, from Darwin's finches to the evolution of hospital superbugs mutating under the selection pressure of human medicine. Evolution is a gradual and statistical process working away with great beauty but no intrinsic purpose. By shuffling the genetic pack through sexual selection and by constantly rewarding random advantages—no matter how small and subtle—with reproductive success, over generations, evolution can lead to great complexity. We humans are so complex that we can think; we should feel astonished and privileged.

But thinking brings doubts. What are we here for? Is there a meaning to it all? Is death the end for the individual? Are we just a bizarre predicament of matter? How do we fit into the vast universe? Inquiring minds could be troubled by such questions, but cleverly we have devised a strategy for containing them; we have invented God. All those questions come under his remit and are safely contained by the occasional ceremony. In the meantime, we carry on expressing all those appetites that have been built into us for sound evolutionary reasons: fighting over territory, killing rivals, organizing ourselves into hierarchies, and sex.

Creationism is a comfort blanket that smothers speculation.

crystals (n.) Lumps of quartz and other crystals have magical properties. Different minerals do different things. Whatever you do, don't crush them up and swallow them with a glass of water. Just being in the same room is efficacious. Pyramids sharpen razor blades too. Hang on to your wallets.

Feng Shui (Chinese – under the canopy of heaven) Fashionable Forgotten Knowledge of the East. Its spread in the West was accelerated by "sick building syndrome"—the realization that some buildings were bad for their inhabitants. Badly adjusted, stale air conditioning, the ion-laden exhaust from the fans of too many computers, sealed windows, perfunctory cleaning, volatile aromatics from carpets, paint, and furniture glue—to say nothing of unremitting stress and working in open-plan partitioned hutches many meters from a window—all made for an unhealthy environment.

Feng Shui gives you spiritual as well as physical health by balancing the forces of *chi* or energy flow within your space. Better activate that brooding southwest corner by moving your filing cabinet. The advantage of Feng Shui for its practitioners (and there are many making a living from it) is that the flow of *chi* changes with time. Just when you think you're perfectly balanced, you have to pay to be assessed again.

grounded (adj.) Not insane. "Centered" can carry the same meaning.

grow as a person (v. phrase) This is a good thing to do. Growing as something else would not be so good.

herbalism (n.) Many plants and herbs contain potent chemicals that pharmaceutical companies spend millions on screening for possible therapeutic effects. Then the chemists try to isolate the active ingredient and if possible synthesize it into a purer form. If you have a headache, for instance, you can take acetylsalicylic acid in the form of aspirin, first made by clever German chemists at Bayer. Alternatively, you could chew rather a lot of the right genus of willow tree. Herbalists prefer the original in all its glorious organic complexity and its hard-to-calibrate dosage. In part this is because the knowledge they have acquired about the medicinal qualities of herbs is old and thus to be revered. There is also a strong prejudice in favor of anything "**natural**." For sound evolutionary reasons, many plants contain substances that are poisonous to creatures that would eat them. Next time you visit a garden center, remember that you are surrounded by toxins.

holistic (adj.) Now something of an all-purpose New Age word, "holistic" was originally applied to medicine in the sense that the whole person, body and soul integrated into one, was to be treated, and not just some fragment of the body that may have misbehaved. Now we can read of holistic management and even holistic rice. Holistic has become a sort of verbal blessing awarded to a wide range of New Age goodies.

homeopathy (n.) Invented in the early nineteenth century by Samuel Hahnemann, a German physician, homeopathy rests on two ideas. The first is that like cures like. In other words, if you mimic the symptoms of an ailment with something that induces a similar condition (for example, by taking a pyretic when you already have a fever), you will brace your own immune system and thereby encourage your body to fix itself. The second is that dilution can enhance the efficacy of curative agents. The dilution is accompanied by a special form of shaking called succession. The dilution of the active agent can be extraordinary. One cubic centimeter of tincture mixed with a liter of water produces a ratio of 1 in 10^3. Repeating that process ten times—and many remedies are diluted as often as thirty times—reduces the ratio to 1 in 10^{33}. In other words, it is unlikely that a single atom of the original remains in any particular cubic centimeter of solution. Homeopaths explain this by saying that the water has somehow been imprinted with the memory of the original. Such an effect would require a whole new notion of causality and a rewriting of physics. (There are similar immense dilutions in Ayurvedic treatments like urine therapy, though in that case some would argue it is a good thing.)

Physics is evolving and most professional scientists have learned not to be doctrinaire, but to date no rigorous studies have found any benefit from homeopathy. There is no good proof that homeopathy works except as a placebo. This is not an effect to be disparaged, however. We all feel better if somebody sympathetic takes an interest. A kindly and empathetic homeopath armed with hundreds of tiny, veggie-sounding bottles can probably do wonders for a host of minor psychosomatic ailments. If it brings comfort and you can afford it, why not? Just be sure not to rely on it as an alternative treatment for anything serious.

karma (Sanskrit – work or action) In the Hindu tradition this is the principle that one's deeds have consequences worthy of reward or punishment in a subsequent life or incarnation. Though embraced in the West as a kind of stoned fatalism (think of Kerouac's *The Dharma Bums*), its hippy proponents missed the point, for karma represents a moral law of cause and effect. If you have led a good life, you may progress through more and more sublime incarnations. It's an attractive idea.

There is not an atom of credible evidence that we have access to any life other than the one we are leading. Shouldn't we just get on with it as intensely as we can?

ley lines (np.) Just as bunnies will wear a track in the grass by always taking the same route, so will men. Ley lines are the just about visible remnants of ancient paths connecting prehistoric burial grounds, Stone Age villages, and even the odd henge. They have been interpreted as Earth Magic; strange conduits of energy. The spiritual powers of ley lines have led believers to ascribe great importance to the points where several of them meet. Recently in the UK, a man bought a hut in Dartmoor for £82,000 on the understanding that a ley line runs right through it.

messages from the dead (np.) In different forms humankind—via shamans, signs in the sky, voices in our heads—has been receiving these for thousands of years. In the nineteenth century, spiritualism was popular. Mediums were people especially sensitive to messages "from the other side," and with the help of a trance state, the right atmospheric setting, and some discreet financial support, they could often get in touch with someone recently departed from our world "into the next." More recently such messages have found expression through contemporary channels. Voices of the dead have been heard, for example, on the phone or in the static hiss of long distance radio transmissions.

The content of the messages—and the fact that they exist at all—is comforting, especially to the lonely and grief-stricken. Woody Allen once said that some people seek immortality through their work, but that he preferred to achieve it by not dying. Mortality is not a bundle of laughs, but isn't it more dignified to face up to the human condition honestly, bleak though it is, without clinging to sham consolations?

Mother Shipton (proper n.) A.k.a. Ursula Sonthiel Shipton (b. Yorkshire, 1488). Mother Shipton was a seer. Apparently she was hideously ugly and her face glowed so brightly that you could see by it at night. She is supposed to have predicted all kinds of things (including that the world would end in 1881). Although it has been revealed that many of her prophecies were written after the event, or were nineteenth-century inventions (the editor of her biography had fun), there is still a core of believers who maintain that she must have had some strange gift. There's no smoke without fire, you see.

nature (n.) **natural** (adj.) The great literary critic William Empson identified eleven different meanings for "nature" and "natural" in *King Lear*. Webster's dictionary has fourteen definitions for the adjective "natural." Among other things, "natural" can mean appropriate, harmonious, fitting, free from artifice, organic, found in the environment, part of the order of things that should obtain, innocent, free from institutional convention, having a character specified by innate qualities, not man-made, not miraculous or supernatural, reflecting man's inner essence...

Nature and natural are hugely multivalent hurrah words; all their positive connotations are deployed by the copywriters of the New Age. "Natural" mineral water, for example, enjoys all the favorable meanings, though it is natural only in the sense that the artifice of man kicks in after the environment has provided it for free. See also **water**.

New Age advertisements will often try to have it both ways by invoking nature and the impressive jargon of science. A recent herbal cure for hay fever, for example, makes a virtue of its natural properties and the fact that it contains cyclic AMP (adenosine monophosphate), the effects of which include inhibition of mast cell degranulation and reduced histamine release. Take one to three daily.

Arsenic is natural. So is the HIV virus.

Nostradamus (Latin name of Michel de Nostredame, 1503–66) This ambitious French physician practiced in Agen and Lyon. Around 1547, he set himself up as an astrologer and prophet and later published two collections of rhyming quatrains, *The Centuries*, that contained predictions. On these his reputation as a prescient seer with paranormal powers still rests. The quatrains themselves were expressed in enigmatic and obscure language. People have interpreted his verses in many ways, for they are ambiguous enough to sustain various readings. The Second World War, the invention of genetic engineering, the assassination of President Kennedy, the prospects for the marriage of a soccer player…all these are foretold, according to enthusiasts, by a study of the quatrains. Interestingly, the accuracy of Nostradamus's predictions only becomes apparent retrospectively. Tooled up with the knowledge of what happened, you can go back to the text after the event and realize with sudden comprehension what he must have meant. A lively Nostradamus industry flourishes to this day.

numerology (n.) The mystical study of numbers using ancient knowledge from Arabic, Jewish, and Chinese sources. In the Chinese tradition, even numbers are *yin* and represent the terrestrial realm, whereas odd numbers have a *yang* quality and are divine or celestial. (According to ancient Chinese beliefs the universe is governed by opposing but complementary principles—*yin* which is female, damp, and earth-bound, and *yang* which is male and heavenly. A balance between these two forces is essential for a good and healthy life.) Numerologists believe that the numbers can be a source of divination.

There's a terrible confusion in numerology between the world and the labels we attach to it. The labels are more easily manipulable.

Visualize some birds sitting in a tree. An observer might recognize them as sparrows. Whether or not the observer is an expert in identifying bird species makes no difference to the birds, which are unaware of the name agreed for them by a hominid species with a classification mania. The identification process is a tiny, private mental event in the brain of a passing biped. If the observer imputed any other characteristics to them, such as charm or noisiness—or indeed "seven-ness"—the same would apply. Only a numerate human being can count that group of tweeters. The occult quality of their number exists in the mind of an observer in possession of a numbering system. The birds would be the same if the observer did not exist, chose a different notation or didn't bother to count them at all. Numerology is an artifact entirely generated by a language we have devised to describe certain aspects of the world. It's intricate but dumb.

organic (adj.) A major hurrah word of the New Age and one which has many meanings. Organic chemistry investigates those processes found in living systems and the spectacular ability of carbon to combine with other elements, especially hydrogen, nitrogen, oxygen, and phosphorus. Organic chemistry is not in opposition to inorganic chemistry; it became a discipline in its own right simply because there is so much of it.

Organic food seems like a tautology—for how could it not be organic? Organic food cannot be produced by factory farming methods and is accordingly more expensive. A large-scale investigation undertaken by Britain's Food Standards Agency (a "position paper" published in 2004) found no health benefit in terms of food safety or nutritional value from eating organic food. The Agency faced a barrage of criticism, some of it on methodology and much on ideological grounds from those who argued that the study was conducted by a government body in thrall to agribusiness.

In the grim business of food and supplement retailing, the word "organic" has been claimed by various certification bodies who license its use to those who meet certain elaborately defined standards. In this context the word "organic" is a commercially valuable mark of accreditation, and one that is fought over as fiercely as in any other business. Some of the campaigns of the organic movement are profoundly sane, however. Do we really need snowpeas imported overnight by Boeing 747 from Kenya? There are many thousands of food miles entailed in creating the typical western meal, and every one represents an irrevocable consumption of energy with all its attendant pollution.

There is no copyright in words belonging to the public lexicon. (That is why traders try to protect their trademarks with snappy misspellings like "Kwik" or "Supa.") Anybody can describe anything "**natural**" as organic and thereby hope to conjure up a picture of sun-dappled greenery, healing harmony, and nut-brown Wise Ones, steeped in ancient lore, pottering about the primal forest looking for rare fungi. Try to imagine a windblown industrial estate instead. Chemicals are chemicals whether found in a tree or manufactured in a retort.

pendulum (n.) Find a weight (brass and crystal are good), tie it to a piece of string—though a golden thread of silk shows a greater sense of theater. Hold the resulting pendulum in your hand (obviously it helps if you are an adept) and set it moving over something you wish to interrogate. It might be a lock of hair or a map. Then you ask questions, and the direction of the swing will tell you the answers. Ho hum.

Rapture, The (n.) The ecstatic bliss that some fundamentalist Christians believe will be experienced by the chosen at the End of Times. It is said that George W. Bush is among their number. There is an apocalyptic nip in the air. The End of Times is not far off. See also **creationism**.

reflexology (n.) An ancient therapy based on the principles of Chinese medicine. The idea is that an image of the body, including the internal organs, can be represented by zones on the foot. Chinese medicine holds that many ailments are the result of energy (*chi*) blockage, so massage and manipulation of the foot can help to unblock those parts of the body to which the areas of the foot correspond.

There is some evidence that having your tootsies massaged in this way is helpful for stress-related disorders. As with much New Age Bullshit, it would be harmless fun if only it did not overclaim.

Roswell (proper n.) Aliens crash-landed at Roswell, New Mexico, in 1947. Years before I worked in the book business and encountered Roswell as a publishing phenomenon, I met an American Air Force man in a pub in Teddington, West London, who assured me that it was true. He knew one of the marines, a man apparently selected for his toughness and lack of imagination, who guarded the bunker where the alien's body was kept. Or maybe he knew a marine who knew a marine…

Once a story is repeated often enough, it seems to take on a life of its own. Periodic inquiries, formal investigations, opening the files, any amount of nay-saying—all are to no avail. This is a story we want to believe. If the USAF spokesmen issue a weary denial more sharply worded than usual, the believers interpret their vehemence as confirmation. They must have something to hide.

If the standard of proof is set high, it is impossible to establish a negative—after all, how many counter-examples would be enough? The logical beauty of cover-up theories is that they can never be refuted.

Voynich Manuscript (n.) This is an intriguing object, a medieval codex that surfaced in Prague when it was sold to Rudolph II of Bohemia in the seventeenth century. It is believed to be much older, possibly the work of Roger Bacon, "Dr Mirabilis," the thirteenth-century Franciscan scholar. After many changes of ownership (it belonged for some years to a Mrs.

Voynich), it ended up in Yale's rare book collection. The Voynich Manuscript is illustrated—and the illustrations suggest that it contains knowledge about herbalism, biology, and cosmology. Unfortunately the text is hand-written in a secret script that nobody, not excluding some formidable crypt-analysts, has ever been able to decode. This impenetrability allows enthusiasts to project their own theories and preoccupations upon it with-out fear of definitive contradiction. The Voynich Manuscript is a genuinely curious artifact, but it has been made to support an unsustainable weight of fruitcake.

water (n.) Water, H_2O, is the most common molecular compound on the surface of the Earth and essential for life. A huge range of other elements and compounds are soluble in it, and we humans have evolved in such a way that we can taste tiny traces of them. Water with a lot of dissolved calcium or magnesium is called "hard" and tends to form insoluble com-pounds with soap. We soften it by replacing those ions with sodium or potassium. Unusually, the solid form of water is less dense than the liq-uid—hence the fact that ice floats. Water is wonderful stuff and for such a simple compound it is surprisingly complex. But although we can dissolve stuff in it, it cannot be "energized."

Mineral water picks up traces of solutes as it percolates slowly through the ground. Then it is either pumped up or, more conveniently, gravity makes it bubble to the surface at the spring line. After the water is filtered, carbon dioxide may be injected into it to make it fizzy ("sparkling") and a giant bottling plant puts it into plastic bottles of different capacities convenient for the various markets at which it is aimed. (A dollar is the going rate for a small bottle to consume with your sandwich.)

The plastic bottles themselves leach into the water minute quantities of phthalates (plasticizers that may have a disruptive effect on the endocrine system). Hundreds of millions of bottles are discarded world-wide every day. Burning them (unless in controlled incinerators) releases polycyclic aromatic hydrocarbons (PAHs), a dangerous and possibly carcinogenic class of chemicals, and small amounts of the deadly poison, dioxin. Throwing the bottles away means that most of them end up in landfill sites where they take millennia to degrade.

There are fantastic claims made by certain water manufacturers (would "bottlers" be a more apt word?). Some waters (note that plural, suggesting diversity) are alleged to enhance athletic or intellectual ability. These virtues are reflected in the price. By all means buy it for the taste, if those minute traces of mineral solutes appeal to your palate (though you should be getting all you need from your diet), but scoff at all that marketing depicting long-limbed, sexy youngsters with beautiful complexions and dazzling teeth. Water is water.

Clean, fresh water is in short supply. The strategists tell us that it will be the cause of twenty-first-century resource wars. In health food stores and smart bars in the West, we can pay several dollars per liter for something of which (the World Health Organization tells us) over 1.2 billion people lack an adequate supply.

PART SEVEN

A Brief Burble about Logical Bullshit

Is to dispute well, logic's greatest end? Affords this art no greater miracle?

—Christopher Marlowe, *Dr. Faustus*

English is awash with words and phrases that suggest that the speaker has established a logical connection between a proposition or series of propositions and what follows. "Hence…therefore…thus…and…not…if…then…accordingly…anybody but a complete wonk will agree…the result is…" All these expressions are what philosophers call "logical operators." Because words in a real language cannot be separated from their emotional hangers-on, it is impossible to tease out the nice distinctions between the various forms of logical connection that can be linked by such operators. To overcome that difficulty philosophers have devised "symbolic logic," in which letters substitute for propositions and symbols replace everyday notions like conjunction or implication.

Implication, for example, can be strong or weak. If A implies B, and A is the case, then B follows. Strong implication would suggest that if A implies B, then if B is not the case then A is also untrue. (If "it is raining" implies the streets are wet, then if the streets are not wet then it's not raining.) Various forms of symbolic logic work with different formal rules.

By now you are probably thinking that philosophers must be irritating people to live with and should get out more. However, symbolic logic has one gorgeous virtue: it allows you to look at the pattern of an argument without being distracted by whether it represents an opinion about the world with which you concur. You can just consider whether the shape of the logic holds good. Actual examples cloud the question. If all cats are gray, and Fleabag is a cat, then Fleabag is gray. In reality, of course, lots of cats are not gray so we risk falling into a wrangle about breeds of cats and their characteristic fur colors. But if all As are B, and X is an A, then X is also B. Abstraction reveals the logic; the validity of the proposition is not in doubt.

But what good is it? Just looking at the construction of an argument can be revealing. For instance, in the example above it is logical to say that X is B if, and only if, *all* As are B and X is definitely an A. It is not a valid inference if only some As are B. (Some cats are gray. Fleabag is a cat. Therefore…well, nothing really can be said about the color of Fleabag.) The philosophical jargon for this is that you can proceed from a universal (a generalization about all) to an existential (an individual case)—but not the other way around. Think of how often we hear that latter version in political argument. Some people in this category—screams a tabloid editorial—have this quality (scroungers on the system perhaps); this person belongs in this category, therefore he too is a bastard scrounger on the system.

A common expression of this fallacy is generalizing from one to all. We can read it frequently in the press. This person has this attribute, therefore all such people have this attribute. The argument may be disguised with emotive accretions: the individual is an egregious example (an immigrant perhaps with three wives, six kids, and an up-market Mercedes). Rather than state baldly that all immigrants fall into the same category, the journalist will cleverly present the case as typical and thus characteristic of a whole class of people (the universal in logic). The inadequacy of this reasoning becomes clear if you recast it in symbolic logic.

Another, more subtle sleight of hand is performed when a politician seeking your vote makes an inference by which he or she maintains that various causes have as their logical consequence some state of affairs which you also believe to be the case. That could be some terribly amorphous truism with which it is hard to disagree. You know the kind of thing: the pressures on family values, the harsh competitiveness of the world, the excessive volume of government regulation… The trick is that some or all of the causal factors listed may be factitious, but nevertheless they have played their part in an argument which led to a sympathetic conclusion, and because it is one with which you agree you tend to perceive the whole inference as valid. Later in the same speech the politician can refer back to those causal factors as if they have been established beyond question, for did we not all nod sagely as he or she wound their way to this woolly opinion? In symbolic logic we can see the pattern. A, B, C, and D imply Y. Y is the case. A and B do seem to imply Y. However, C is stretching things a bit and D has nothing to do with the issue at all. Not Y does not suggest not D, for instance.

We cannot ignore the possibility that when a politician looks to camera and says, "This follows as night follows day…" he or she may be right. The logic could be impeccable in the sense that it follows from the first premise. Logic is about following a set of formal rules whereby propositions can validly be derived from others, rather like mathematics. (Boolean algebra and set theory are mathematical expressions of logic.) We have to be on our guard not just against sloppy logic, but also accurate logic, for it may well be that the initial assumption from which the argument flows with such rigor is a colossal and mischievous illusion.

PART EIGHT

Fossil Words and Tired Old Images

Drawing on my fine command of language, I said nothing.
—Robert Benchley

The longevity of words and images is remarkable. Many a PhD thesis must have been written on the subject. My guess is that words endure if they meet two conditions: they are widely enough in circulation in the first place and they are useful. They fall into desuetude when they cease to have a commonly understood reference, but they remain on the landscape like those rocks, dropped by retreating glaciers, unconnected to anything in the landscape for miles around.

For this reason the great *Oxford English Dictionary* is more than just an amazing collection of words. It is a source of history, gravid not only with contemporary vocabulary but also objects and ideas that have all but disappeared from the world. Who now needs futtocks (the curved ribs of a sailing ship) or the phlogiston theory of combustion? But we can still be tense, and thus "on tenterhooks," even though that fabric stretching device was superseded many decades ago. Technological words seem to survive particularly well. Images from the age of sail and steam are still used by people too young ever to have seen a steam locomotive, never mind a clipper.

There is nothing wrong with these old words, and much guiltily obsessive pleasure to be had in recalling their origins. But they are tired. Once they evoked vivid images and added color to conversation and writing. Now they are in their dotage and flaccid. We need a new generation of inventive English speakers and writers to revive the stock lest we all start to sound like corporate footwork artists on a particularly dull day.

There must be thousands of words that qualify as fossils; here are just a few.

balls on a brass monkey (np.) As in "freeze the balls off a brass monkey." Disappointingly, the etymologist and all-around word maestro, Michael Quinion, maintains this is not a marine expression at all. (In engineering, a monkey is a frame and the balls are cannon balls that would roll off the frame when the extreme cold made it contract.) Quinion thinks it is more likely that the brass monkey was one of the set that famously saw, heard, or spoke no evil. Such brass statuettes were common as a jocular decoration. They haunted those nicotine-beige dining rooms in bed and breakfast hotels by the seaside well into the 1960s.

beg the question (v.) The magisterial Fowler, the authority on English usage, maintains that on the subject of the split infinitive the Anglophone world can be divided into four. There are those who know what it is, and care, and those who know but do not care. Then there are people who think they know, but are wrong, and a large number who neither know nor care.

Much the same can be said about "begging the question" except that those who know its original meaning also write intemperate letters to the newspapers or National Public Radio about its misuse. (How easily such correspondents are moved to anger.)

Begging the question once applied to logical argument. You begged the question by assuming the truth of that which you wanted to prove. This can be a deliberate technique: you might be able to demonstrate a paradox at the end of your chain of reasoning if the assumption in question were to turn out not to be the case. On the other hand it may be sloppy. For instance, you could argue in favor of capital punishment on the grounds it diminishes the general crime rate by pointing out how beneficial such a reduction would be for society at large. In that example, you have begged the question by assuming that capital punishment does reduce the overall crime rate, the very proposition that needs to be true if your argument holds good.

The expression, however, sounds as if it ought to mean something along the lines that here is a question urgently prompted by circumstance, one that is crying out to be answered. So many people use it this way that I think its meaning will inevitably change. Anguished letters from pedants will continue for generations.

bitter end, the (n.) A marine expression. The "bitts" are the inboard end of an anchoring cable, so by the time you get to the bitter end, you have played out every last inch. The expression works well because of the more common meaning of "bitter." It sounds as if you're bent on going on regardless of the pain.

blow one's stack (v.) A stack was a tall chimney over a furnace. It could also be the funnel of a steam ship or steam locomotive. Blowing one's stack was either a catastrophic industrial accident (blowing in the sense of blowing up) or something nearly as dramatic—venting all the pressure from a boiler up the chimney in order to avoid an explosion. See also **get up steam**.

break ranks (military) Until the nineteenth century, generals tended to draw up their soldiers into ranks and files. The rank—not for nothing the same word as for hierarchical status—was a horizontal formation and could be many deep. Musketeers were often in two ranks, so that one line could be firing while the other was reloading. Breaking ranks—for instance in the face of the enemy—was not just cowardly but could endanger the lives of all your fellows. "Closing ranks" was desperately important for the same reason. Now it just means keeping expediently quiet.

clink (n.) Prison. This was an actual jail (1151–1780) in south London notorious for its dankness, rats, and brutality.

close to the wind (marine) Sailing by tacking as nearly as possible into the wind is a feat needing skill and seamanship. It is tricky and difficult, which may explain why the expression came to mean edging up to the very limits of legality as defined by the rules.

cock and bull (adj.) A cock and bull story is rambling and improbable. The *OED* cites the earliest reference in Robert Burton's *Anatomy of Melancholy* in 1621 ("Some men's whole delight is to talk of Cock and Bull over a pot"). The reference is to sententious, rustic geezers who have had a beer or three and spin unlikely yarns using what would then have been understood to be wildly disparate creatures. There's not much a cock and a bull could do together; they have little in common apart from being unequivocally male.

copper-bottomed (marine) A wooden hull was sheathed in copper to protect it from the depredations of the teredo worm and the build-up of barnacles and weeds that would slow its passage through the water. First introduced into the British Navy in 1761, a copper-bottomed ship of the line was the most fearsome technology of the time; the expression soon migrated to mean well-made and certain.

cut and dried (adj.) If you went to a herbalist, you could buy something fresh if you were lucky and the herbalist had just been out collecting. More likely, you would come away with herbs that were already cut and dried.

decimate (v.) Reduce *by* a tenth—not *to* a tenth. Much misused as a synonym for annihilate, it was actually a savage managerial technique in the time of the Roman legions whereby every tenth man was murdered to keep the others in line. Amoral executives still use a similar device to frighten the workforce. There's nothing like a blood sacrifice to demonstrate to the powers-that-be that a manager is on the case.

dial [a number] (v.) A minor example of a verb that one day will be the subject of a scholarly footnote. Only the owners of a self-consciously retro-chic phone need dial, for it is a rotary action. The rest of us have been prodding buttons for decades. The verb "punch" is often used, but it sounds awkward. We use a finger not a fist. Something similar has happened to "pull up" in a car, an echo of the time of reins and horses.

flash in the pan, a (np.) An image from musketry. The priming powder in the pan would ignite but not set off the charge that propelled the ball from the barrel. Some scholars suggest that a flash in the pan derives from panning for gold, but as the primer on a flintlock was called the flashpan, musketry seems more likely. Either way, the picture was once vivid.

forlorn hope (np.) Forlorn means lost and, by extension, morally adrift and rather despairing, but "forlorn hope" has an unusual military derivation from the Dutch *verloren hoop*—literally a lost troop. It was a picked body of men sent to the front like skirmishers to begin the attack. The *OED* quotes Digges, the Elizabethan astronomer (1570): "He must also so order the Forlorn hope in ye front of hys Battayle with new supplies."

get up steam (v.), **all steamed up** (adj.) Proper trains were pulled by steam locomotives and not by diesels or diesel-electrics; engines with all the charisma of a dead pigeon. A Pacific class 4-6-2 steam locomotive weighed in at 128 tons and was a joy to behold. Steam pressure could be as high as 245 pounds per square inch—seventeen times atmospheric pressure. The massive boiler would have to be tended and stoked for hours to reach that level. And when it got there, steam would vent from valves and cylinders so the whole machine would hiss like some iron dragon; the *clank-clank* cycling of the valve gear sounded like mechanical lungs. To be ready in the morning, the fire had to be kept going all night so that the flue and boiler pipes would draw properly. If you were close to an engine letting off steam, you would jump. The noise was frightening—something between a piercing shriek and an explosion. In a high-arched Victorian station, the steam could condense as a warm, sooty rain. All these associations have been lost in time, but the steam metaphors live on.

Gold Standard, the (np.) This expression has come to mean the standard of excellence by which others are measured. It's an interesting example of how words revert to their base meaning once the original reference has faded. The Gold Standard was an economic system whereby the price of gold was pegged to each member country's currency within a fairly narrow range. The system offered stability of exchange rates but at the cost of national control of monetary policy. It also played havoc with the money supply. Britain adopted the system in 1821 but suspended gold payments in 1914. The Gold Standard was reintroduced in 1925, but it finally collapsed for good during the Depression of the 1930s and is unlikely ever to return.

In theory, while it was operating, you could zip down to your country's national bank and exchange your paper currency for gold. It has a primitive appeal.

kibosh (n. and v.) The *OED* states that the origin of this word is obscure but it might be Anglo-Yiddish costermonger's slang. An American source suggests that it was a term for adding cement or plaster to a form, though quite how this came to mean to interfere with or generally sabotage is not clear. It is such a lovely word, mysterious and almost onomatopoeic.

learn the ropes (marine) A ship of the line at the time of the Napoleonic Wars carried over a mile of rope. An able seaman was expected to know what to do with every inch.

lock, stock, and barrel (military) All the bits of the musket, in other words.

loose cannon (marine) A big cannon was massively heavy. It was anchored by ropes and draglines to limit its recoil when being fired. Loose during a battle or in rough sea, it could roll about, crushing people and equipment and possibly smashing a hole in the wooden hull. A loose cannon could imperil the whole ship.

milk train, the (np.) Sometimes confused with the gravy train, the milk train ran appallingly early, usually before dawn. The train carried milk in enormous tanks into the city where it was distributed to local dairies and thence to front doorsteps by milkmen. The milk run was done every day except Sunday and became synonymous with something routine.

Once a week, the milkman would collect the money owed to the dairy. A rich mythology built up about impecunious housewives offering the milkman services in lieu of payment, and this led to many jokes—which would now need scholarly apparatus—about famously horny milkmen suffused with honorable exhaustion by the end of their rounds.

newfangled (adj.) Do any of us know what the verb "to fangle" means? The *OED* gives various meanings—to fashion, to fabricate, to trick out, to trifle. As a noun, a "fangle" was a fantastic, foppish, or silly contrivance, especially of clothing. The word cries out for reintroduction.

on the nail (adv.) This image for prompt payment comes from the floor in the Royal Exchange in Bristol, southwest England. Until the abolition of the slave trade in 1807, ships from Bristol would sail down to West Africa with goods for trade, buy slaves, transport them, packed like logs, to America and the West Indies where they would be sold, and pick up sugar and cotton for the return journey. It was immensely profitable. The "nails" are still there, set in the floor. They are great iron spikes with round, flattened tops like a small table. Paying on the nail meant that the trader would bang down his cash for some transaction on that handy surface.

sell down the river (v.) The river in question was the Mississippi. In the first half of the nineteenth century in America, slaves were sold from the Upper South to the booming cotton and sugar plantations of the Deep South. Slaves were transported downstream to the markets at Natchez and New Orleans.

spick and span (adj.) A spick was a nail and a span a piece of wood, so how did this expression evolve to mean scrumptiously clean and neat?

swashbuckling (adj.) Both parts of this lovely word are obsolete, yet nothing else does as well. To "swash" was to strut one's stuff and swagger about. It's vaguely onomatopoeic, rather like the modern verb "swank" or the slightly old-fashioned noun "swell" in the sense of a pleased-with-himself man about town. A buckler was a small shield. It must be getting on for five hundred years since an authentic swashbuckler could have been spotted drinking a mug of beer and gunpowder.

throw in the towel/sponge (v.) Bare-knuckle boxing was a bloody business that could last for hours, with the number of rounds limited only by the endurance of the fighters. If you were battered insensible, somebody in your corner would toss the bloodstained towel into the ring as a sign that you would not be coming out again for more punishment. Throwing in the towel—still commonly used as a metaphor for giving up or conceding defeat—would have conjured up a very gutsy image.

toss one's hat into the ring (v.) In contrast to **throw in the towel**, this indicated that you were ready for a contest (which could have been wrestling as well as boxing). Feverish gambling on the outcome was part of the gory fun.

umbrage (n.) From Old French and means—inter alia—shadow. The *OED* lists "taking offense, showing resentment" as only its eighth meaning.

white elephant (np.) In India elephants are highly regarded and white ones—being very rare—particularly so. If a maharajah was given one as a present, it would have been impossible to kill surreptitiously even if you could bring yourself to do it. After all, it was semi-sacred, a gift, and the size of, well, an elephant. An elephant may live for a century and take up to fifteen years to train. An adult will eat fifty-five pounds of food per day and needs to be housed somewhere large and strongly built. A bull elephant in full musk is worse than an adolescent boy; it's grumpy and dangerous. Every day the elephant will need to be taken to a lake or river for a cooling wash and scrub. A team of servants, from the mahout to the boy gathering the staggering quantities of poo, would have been employed to look after such an animal.

The difficulty and expense of housing a white elephant must have been a considerable pain in the purse even for a maharajah.

Appendix

The Drake Equation (see **aliens** under New Age and Alternative Bullshit) was developed by Frank Drake of the SETI program (the Search for Extraterrestrial Intelligence) and is designed to estimate the number of intelligent, communicating civilizations there are in our galaxy, the Milky Way. It is impossible to make more than an informed guess about the sum of the variables, but the beauty of the equation is that it provides a formal framework for thinking about the question. By adjusting the values for some of the factors (and there are some brilliant websites that allow you to do this online), you can easily calculate the change in output. The results vary from tens of thousands of technologically advanced cultures down to almost zero. We know that the right conditions have been fulfilled at least once on a planet, for we are living on it.

$$N = N^* fp\ ne\ fl\ fi\ fc\ fL$$

N* represents the number of stars in the galaxy, estimated at around 250 billion.

fp is the fraction of stars with planetary systems. Estimates vary from 20 to 50 percent.

ne is the number of planets that are capable of sustaining life.

fl is the fraction of those planets on which life has evolved.

fi is the fraction of fl where intelligent life has appeared.

fc is the fraction of fi that is sufficiently advanced to communicate.

fL is the fraction of the planet's life during which such civilizations flourish. (On Earth we have been sending out radio waves for only a century or so, and some pessimists believe that we will destroy ourselves in short order.)

Afterword

Contributing Your Own Bullshit

We live in a world awash with Bullshit. I hope that this volume will make a small contribution to holding back the tide.

Readers are invited to join the battle against bullshit by emailing in prize examples to the website below. Bizarre usages, ugly jargon, and impenetrable waffle are all welcome, but Bullshit damaging to clarity of thought is of particular interest. I will check the site as often as I can but cannot promise to reply to all correspondents. However, any bullshit gleaned from readers that may be published in further editions will be gratefully acknowledged.

Address: www.dobcontributors.com

About the Author

NICK WEBB was a publisher for nearly 30 years before turning to writing. The former managing director of Simon & Schuster UK, he describes his past life as "paddling a small raft across an ocean of bullshit." His biography of his friend Douglas Adams, author of *The Hitchhiker's Guide to the Galaxy,* was published in 2003. Nick is married and lives in East London with his wife and daughter.